DIALOGUES ON
AMERICAN POLITICS

DIALOGUES ON
AMERICAN POLITICS

IRVING LOUIS HOROWITZ
Rutgers University

SEYMOUR MARTIN LIPSET
Stanford University

New York   OXFORD UNIVERSITY PRESS   1978

Copyright © 1978 by Irving Louis Horowitz
and Seymour Martin Lipset

Library of Congress Cataloging in Publication Data
Horowitz, Irving Louis.
  Dialogues on American politics.

  Edited transcriptions of debates between the authors,
in 1976 and 1977.
    1. United States—Politics and government—1945–
2. United States—Social conditions—1960–   3. Political sociology. I. Lipset, Seymour Martin. II. Title.
JK271.H728   320.9′73′092   78-7872
ISBN 0-19-502449-4
ISBN 0-19-502450-8 pbk.

Printed in the United States of America

To   DAVID RIESMAN
Mentor to us both
on the nature of American life

DIALOGUES ON AMERICAN POLITICS   was an idea first
suggested by Dean Jack C. Buckle of Lycoming College in
Pennsylvania, who subsequently became chairman of the
dialogue series. As he conceived it, major spokesmen in
the social science fields would be invited to debate the key
premises and propositions of their particular fields of interest. Stanley Wilk, a sociologist, and Donald M. Borock, a
political scientist, both of whom were affiliated in the
spring of 1976 with this intercollegiate activity, paired the
authors of this book for one such dialogue.

We would like to express our gratitude to these fine
people not only for their conceptual mapping of this program but for their translation of that initial conception
into a workable program. An authentic dialogue in political
sociology is a rare event, and long overdue.

Since that time our dialogues, now in manuscript form,
have gone through various changes. Suprisingly, even
after two years, most of the changes seem to be cosmetic
rather than substantive—providing evidence for a point,
qualifying hyperbolic language, or eliminating a certain
chattiness the oral form invites but which, when set down
in print, becomes tedious. Helping us every step of the
way were our two remarkable secretaries, Sheila G. Brill
and Brenda W. McLean.

It should be noted that the third dialogue, on the presidency, is much more current, having been prepared in September and October of 1977. We felt, as did our publisher, that an added dialogue on the presidency would be useful not only to update ideas discussed in the first three dialogues but also because of the intrinsic importance of the subject itself. We believed that an examination of the electoral process as a structural entity in American society, over and against the political processes involved in the nominating procedures, might benefit from the particular analytic perspective of our own field of political sociology. Rather than try to blend new wine into old, however, we decided to duplicate our earlier process and tape a fourth session during the calm after the electoral storm that would specifically address problems of the presidency.

We have been cognizant of the problems involved in this format and have done everything possible to overcome its limitations. First, there is the problem of the essentially informal nature of the dialogue in contrast to the more formal requirements of the essay or monograph. While we chose to retain the essential liveliness of this oral form, it has not been retained at the price of reducing scholarly dialogue to witty repartee. Second, too often dialogues are mere monologues. Nothing better illustrates this proclivity than the venerated Socratic dialogues themselves, wherein the wisdom of the party of the first part stands in clear distinction to the foolishness of the parties of the second and third parts. A third problem can arise in the dialogue form when discourse takes place between people of disparate backgrounds or ideological persuasions. Rather than a dialogue, something more akin to a pair of antipathetic diatribes is produced. And such artificial constructs end up like two ships passing in the night; rarely, if ever, do they connect either emotionally or intellectually.

Although for many years now we have been representatives of different wings of political sociology and different professional forces, both of us have been cognizant of the need to maintain a personal dialogue based on evidence, information, and, above all, the good will that comes with friendship. These emotions are underwritten by a common purpose and the belief that the field of political sociology has much to recommend itself as a major pivot in twentieth-century social science. We sincerely hope that this dialogue in four parts provides a persuasive framework for others to pursue these themes and eventually to enlarge the scope and enrich the contents of modern political sociology.

IRVING LOUIS HOROWITZ,
Rutgers University

SEYMOUR MARTIN LIPSET,
Stanford University

November 1, 1977

CONTENTS

I. POLITY

LIPSET Today we want to start this dialogue by discussing ideology in politics in America. This is presumably an appropriate time to do so. To understand the general role of ideology, or rather of different ideological groupings in American society, one must first recognize that if we use the word "party" in the sense in which people talk about parties in Europe, then the United States does not have a two-party system.

European parties, even in Britain, which has had a two-party system until recently, are organizations that have a central core of interest or ideology around which people gather. The American parties, as many political scientists and others have noted, are essentially coalitions—coalitions of often highly disparate groupings drawn together by interest as well as ideology.

In most European countries that have proportional representation multiparty election systems, a coalition of parties will come together after an election to form a government. It is often the only way they can create a majority in Parliament. In the United States, because our constitution requires that we elect one person as president or governor, we have a concealed multiparty system, one that produces two coalition candidates. We have two coalition parties, both formed during the preelection period, while the Europeans have many parties that form postelection coalitions. In this context I would suggest that in the United States today we have, roughly speaking, five different tendencies—five different factions or ideological groupings—running from right to left. To understand these, one must see that issues in this country cross two dimensions that are fairly simple ones.

One is the economic dimension—economic liberalism or conservatism, or, if you will, stratification. Politically, this involves such issues as the progressive income tax, social security, socialized medicine, planning to prevent economic depressions, and the like. In America conservatives are generally opposed to state intervention in the economy or to efforts to redistribute income. Liberals, people on the left, are in favor of such actions. People may, of course, vary as to how far to the left or to the right they lean. The second dimension, often referred to as the social dimension to distinguish it from the economic one, involves positions on such matters as civil rights for minority groups, civil liberties for dissident political groups, rights for homosexuals, law and order, crime, sexual permissiveness, abortion, pornography, patriotism, military budgets—all of which fall in this complex of social or noneconomic issues. People here may also be positioned as more liberal or conservative.

These two dimensions correlate, hang together, to some extent, in that people who are economic liberals tend to be social liberals, and vice versa. But the correlation is not absolute. Many *are* liberal on one and conservative on the other. Accounting for the most frequently observed combinations, one finds four logical groupings—people who are consistent liberals or consistent conservatives on both dimensions, and those who are liberal on one and conservative on the other. Empirically, there is in fact a fifth grouping, because the social conservatives divide up to some extent in their attitudes on race. There are groups or individuals who are social conservatives on most issues except the race issue. There are others who are social conservatives and racists—they are essentially against doing much to improve the situation for blacks and other minority groups. There are, therefore, at least five factions.

A look at the positions of these factions in the party system helps explain recent developments. The consistent conservatives (people who are economic conservatives and social conservatives) make up the Goldwater-Reagan wing of the Republican party. Those who are consistent liberals on economic and social issues constitute the pro-McGovern, "New Politics" wing of the Democratic party. Those who are economic liberals and social conservatives—the position of the dominant wing in the AFL-CIO, epitomized by the views of George Meany—form the core of the moderate wing of the Democratic party identified with Henry (Scoop) Jackson. Some who hold this position are, however, racist, and since the leaders of this faction are antiracist, there is a subfaction composed of Wallace Democrats. (Wallace also has appealed to racists among the consistent conservatives.) Those who are economically conservative but socially liberal are the liberal Republicans, identified with Nelson Rockefeller and Charles Percy.

The five major issue publics differ, of course, in their size and strength. Since they do not run separate candidates in the same election, it is impossible to assign precise numbers to each. Looking at poll data, however, one finds that the largest of these five groupings is the economically liberal–socially conservative one, exemplified by Meany and based to a large extent on the trade union movement. The outcome of recent elections then may be understood in terms of the coalitions created by the two parties. The nominee who wants to get elected has to somehow form a majority by attracting substantial blocs of voters from these five different factions. The winner will be largely determined, in my opinion, by whether the economic or the social issues command the vote of the larger section of the electorate.

Stratification issues tend to be seen as primary, more salient, when we have downswing economic troubles (recession), which breed unemployment. The Democrats will have appeal to all the economic liberals, thus uniting the New Politics social liberals with the Meany–Jackson social conservatives. In 1976, in a period of moderate unemployment and high inflation, Carter had a narrow victory by successfully appealing to both wings. On the other hand, when economic conditions are good, when most people are assured of employment, at that point many will respond to noneconomic moral or social concerns. Such periods benefit the Republican party.

The Republican party is clearly most advantaged by a period of full employment and moderate inflation. Republican successes in the elections of the 1950s, of 1968, and of 1972 all occurred under such conditions, with candidates emphasizing social issues. The GOP majorities were obtained by securing a significant vote from people who were economic liberals—people who favored aspects of the welfare state but who were more concerned about moral, cultural, and national interest matters.

These generalizations are obviously oversimplified. I have ignored the impact of unanticipated major events and scandals. Foreign policy issues, such as those produced by the Vietnam war, obviously introduced a major upsetting factor in this kind of neat packaging of the five groups I've presented. Nevertheless, thinking in these terms is basic to understanding the nature of the American party system and how different ideologies and interest groups mesh to elect governments.

HOROWITZ   The American two-party system consists of a dominant (Democratic) majority party and a minority opposition (Republican) party. As a result, America has an unusual two-party system, but one in which the party apparatus has an autonomous reality. The structure of party affairs is such that it would be a mistake to think of the American party system simply in terms of coalitions. Coalitions based on considerations of class, race, and religion are indeed necessary if a party is to win national elections. But when the larger national pattern is looked at in terms of a legislative framework, over and against an executive framework, there can be no doubt that the Democratic party is, in fact, the majority party. This profoundly limits its ad hoc coalitional behavior. Electoral coalitions are less pronounced in legislative districts than in executive struggles: coalitions take place at national presidential primaries and become especially decisive in presidential politics. That is why presidential candidates from the minority Republican party, being less encumbered by populist and elitist varieties of liberalism, can, under special conditions, emerge victorious in national elections.

We tend to assume that the executive branch encapsulates the meaning of the political process. From my own vantage point, the legislative branch, more than the so-called imperial presidency, defines the fabric and the texture of American democratic political life. The legislative branch of government gives substance and reality to the party system over and above any temporary coalition at the executive levels. While I agree with Professor Lipset that there is such a phenomenon as coalition politics, I see that phenomenon more narrowly—as coalitional presidential politics. And such coalitions do not vitiate the fact of party life in America, nor the reality of Democratic party majorities at congressional and gubernatorial levels. For despite vast sectional and ideological differences within the Democratic party, it remains the fulcrum of activity for trade unionists, blacks, Mexican-Americans, minority groups, the Jewish population, and the Southern states (which have traditionally been Democratic). This strange collective has given the Democratic party a permanent edge.

American presidential politics is akin to a handicap race. The Democratic party starts with a distinctive voter majority (especially at national levels); whereas the Republican party has a constant, uphill chore of winning elections by moving voters from their registered preferences to their presumed actual interests. A political typology that divides the electorate into ideological divisions—extreme right, moderate right, vital center, moderate left, and extreme left—can too easily overlook the pragmatic necessity of winning hearts and minds by ignoring fine ideological distinctions. Lipset also speaks of distinct racial and nonracial factions within the political right wing. Again, one must be cautious, and appreciate the extent to which attitudes toward race, at least in terms of party politics, are determined more by the desire to win elections than by ideological divisions or racial persuasions. One would imagine that such a position would be axiomatic for Lipset, who, after all, is a major sponsor of the "end of ideology" thesis. And yet, peculiarly enough, his position clings firmly to an ideological definition of party politics in American life.

Let us further examine Lipset's argument. He and a number of his colleagues have argued elsewhere that there is a self-contained group called the "extreme right." They have written about and surveyed this group. Yet, for the most part, members of the so-called extreme right do not see themselves as Lipset sees them. For example, they view themselves as good Americans. They claim to embody traditional American persuasions about work, thrift, morality, and faith. They may score slightly higher on authoritarian scales, but they do not perceive themselves as right-wingers, only as standard-bearers of the American work-ethic.

They are considerably different from left-wingers, who do perceive themselves as part of an organized (or disorganized) opposition. A more accurate overall picture of American political ideology, I believe, is one in which the left sees itself in highly ideological terms; the center, in highly coalitional terms; and the right, as embodying ongoing American virtues and values. Lipset's five elements thus quickly reduce themselves to a triad. This triad, rather than his quintet, is the essence of the instability and the shifting nature of power within American political party life. Electoral coalitions themselves are not enough to win national power; the party in power invariably must capture the high ground of the meaty center. Self-definitions in terms of Americanism or radicalism are disastrous in terms of national politics. To occupy left or right poles is to move to the base of political activism; to control the center is to capture the apex.

What has been the Republican party strategy between 1956 and 1976? Part of it has involved Kevin Phillips's idea of a Southern strategy, which has also meant breaking away a portion of the Democratic "New Deal coalition." The response of the Democratic party has been to resist such an erosion. The Carter phenomenon represents less the restoration of the New Deal phenomenon as it does the final consequence of the voting right act of 1964. It involves reconstructing the Southern tier without alienating the black vote, the minority vote, the Jewish vote, the Northern vote, or trade union support. "Carterism" is New Dealism in the era of black electoral power. It recreates Democratic strength that is coalitional in form, but centrist in content. As a result, there is considerable doubt about Carter's ability to hold such a coalition in check in a post-electoral climate emphasizing political payoffs. Again, it is not so much a question of the fivefold divisions from extreme right to extreme left that is decisive, but rather the tripartite division of right, center, and left; what might be termed fundamentalism, coalitionalism, and radicalism, respectively.

American political life is not symmetrical in either size or shape. The right wing does not view itself as ideological but as the standard-bearer of traditional values. The center does not see itself as opportunistic but as pragmatic and flexible. And the left, precisely because of its critical ideological standpoint, is extremely fragmented, sure only of its animosities. Rather than focus upon the coalitional aspects of American political life, it may be more prudent to come to terms with the political mixtures that, in their components, compel solutions within a two-party framework. The latent task of coalitions within the American party system is not so much to win but to prevent oppositional formations from achieving their ends at the expense of other elements in the coalition. The plethora of interest groups makes possible the monism of party structures in American society.

LIPSET   I would agree with much of what you say, but obviously I must disagree with some of it. First of all, there is no question that the Democratic party is the dominant party, if you will, the majority party. This has been true since some time in the thirties when Franklin Roosevelt was able to transfer support to the Democrats that the Republicans had held previously, through his handling of economic issues. The large majority of the blacks, and as well as many less well-to-do Protestant workers and farmers, shifted from the GOP to the Democrats between 1932 and 1936, and most have remained loyal to their new allegiance.

In recent years a comparison of some attitudinal findings in the opinion polls on partisan identifications suggests a curious anomaly. When the pollsters ask their subjects for their party preference, 40–45 percent say they are Democrats, while 20 percent or less identify themselves as Republican. Of course, these statistics vary a bit with the poll or occasion of the interview. Another 35–40 percent call themselves independents. An examination of party registrations produces a similar distribution—there are many more registered Democrats than Republicans. On the other hand, for some time now when pollsters have asked "Are you a liberal or conservative?" or have requested respondents to rank themselves on a scale from extreme conservative to extreme liberal, more people describe themselves as conservatives than liberals.

The percentages vary somewhat according to the way in which the question is asked, but conservatives invariably outnumber the liberals. Sometimes the ratio is as much as two-to-one; at other times it is four-to-three. Many, 30–35 percent, put themselves in the middle. This finding creates what seems to be the anomaly, that Democrats and conservatives outnumber the Republicans and liberals. These data underlie the recommendations by two leading Republican conservative political strategists, Kevin Phillips and William Rusher, to dissolve the Republican party because the party name is unpopular and is linked in the minds of many voters to unpopular past policies and special interests, particularly big business. They propose the creation of a new party to be called Conservative, based on the assumption that there are many people who call themselves conservatives who would vote for a Conservative party but not for the Republican party.

The Phillips–Rusher proposal, however, ignores the underlying base of the anomoly, which is linked to the factions I discussed earlier. If we attempt to find out why some people call themselves Republicans and others Democrats, it appears that people relate party labels to positions on economic issues. The Democratic party, in the mind of the electorate, stands for Medicare, extension of health insurance, old-age pensions, government planning to hold down unemployment, assistance to the under privileged, and is linked to unions. The Republican party is seen as antistatist, antiactivist, pro-laissez-faire, and allied with big business.

Given the choice, many more people would opt for government to do more for people like themselves or for the underprivileged over the alternative of limited government. The majority view big labor and big business as special interests that ought not receive backing from the state. Fortunately for the Democratic party, unions are seen, to some extent, at least, as benefiting their less affluent mass membership, while big business is perceived as extracting exhorbitant profits for the advantage of their small group of wealthy stockholders. Thus, Democratic links to labor cost them less than Republican ties to business. In any case, unions have many more members—including recently a growing number of white collar workers and professionals—than any other organized politically concerned group. The Democrats benefit as well from being seen as the party of the common man. The Republican party loses by being linked to the elite, to great wealth. The party-linked economic and class images help produce a Democratic majority.

The conservatives lead the liberals, however, because these labels do not carry with them economic or stratification associations. Rather, many people who tell pollsters they are conservatives mean by this that they are for law and order, and for stricter punishment of criminals; that they are against busing; that they favor doing something about pornography; that they are against abortion; that they favor a larger military budget. Not all of these issues but a cluster of this type characterizes the conservative. Obviously, many individuals take the socially conservative position on some issues and the liberal one on others. Still, the terms liberal, moderate, and conservative refer to positions on these kinds of issues. Consequently, some people who may be economically liberal, and hence Democrats, say they are conservative because of their views on these noneconomic issues.

If we look at the social correlates of these views, it seems evident that noneconomic liberalism correlates strongly with education. The less education people have, the more likely they are to be hardliners on issues like pornography, abortion, stiff sentences for lawbreakers, and so forth. On the other hand, poorer people tend to be more liberal on economic issues. These relationships clearly criss-cross and so do not form a neat left, right, and center. These crossing correlations may help explain some seemingly contradictory election results. In the twenty-four years between 1953 and 1973, the Republicans have had the presidency for sixteen of them, the Democrats for only eight. The Democrats, however, have won a majority in Congress in every year but 1952. That year's was the only Congress elected in the Eisenhower-Nixon-Ford presidencies that had a Republican majority.

What seems to be involved here is that when people vote along party lines the Democrats win. Most people, when they vote in Congressional elections (or for state legislators), vote for a party rather than a candidate. The polls indicate that the big majority of the people do not know who their congressperson is, let alone his opponent. Therefore, when they vote in congressional elections, they much more often elect Democrats. This is even more common on the level of state legislatures. As of 1978 the Democrats hold the governorship and both houses in twenty-nine states, while the Republicans have comparable control in only one state, New Hampshire. The GOP has majorities in both houses in only eight states, and seven of these have Democratic governors. Over 90 percent of the mayors of major cities are Democrats. At best, we now have a one and one-half-party system comparable in many ways to that which existed in the early decades of the nineteenth century.

For the GOP, the situation may be even more serious than the election results suggest. The Democrats have been winning in low turnout elections. But the half of the electorate in recent years who has not voted has been preponderantly lower in socioeconomic status than the habitual voters. All the studies of participation agree that the better educated and more well-to-do a person, the more likely he is to register and vote. Less than 40 percent of the lower status groups, like blacks, Chicanos, and poor whites who are Democratic when they do vote, have been voting in city, state, and recently, even presidential contests. If their proportion as voters is increased as a result of changes in election laws that eliminate registration requirements, or because of greater efforts to turn them out, or because of their increased interest in the outcome, the Democratic advantage will increase.

The presidential elections, of course, do help focus attention on issues—the issues of the day—and on the characteristics of the candidates. The Republicans are able to pick up more support in presidential or gubernatorial elections than in the congressional and legislative elections where they are handicapped by being, as Professor Horowitz said, "the minority party." This is the underlying reality. If you take the other point he made, this question of the emotive feeling attached to different ideological labels, there also is no question that he is right. The more conservative wing of the Republicans, described as this country's right wing, suffers from the fact that the term "right wing" is a negative one in the eyes of the great majority. Few people consider themselves "right-wingers." A few years ago an opinion poll asked people to agree or disagree with the statement that they would vote for a right-winger. About half of the people who said at the time that they preferred George Wallace also indicated that they would not vote for a right-winger. This clearly meant that many of the Wallace people did not regard Wallace as a right-winger, so that the application of the label right-winger to him may have lost him considerable support.

The term "right wing" is almost as negative in America as the term Communist. Right-wingers are viewed as un-

American extremists. Left-wingers are clearly not as bad. The term "left" tends to be thought of by many as synonomous with the term "liberal." Conservatism obviously is not an invidious term. Many of the people who think of themselves as conservatives are not ideological in their self-conception. Certainly the centrist Democrats—the Meany kind of people—do not think of themselves in ideological terms. To think consciously in ideological terms in this country is largely a function of education. The opinion poll data indicate that the college-educated population in both parties tend to be more ideological; their attitudes on issues are more consistent and predictable. The college-educated Democrats form the bulk of the McGovern New Politics wing of the party. College-educated Democrats are more likely to be on the left than are less-educated supporters of the party. The same pattern occurs within the Republican party. A considerable percentage of the college-educated Republicans are consistent conservatives.

The less educated in both parties are the less ideological. They are more oriented toward specific issues that concern them and are more likely to hold contradictory positions. Thus, it appears that the less-committed occupy the center. These phenomena suggest that in a two-party system both parties should compete for the center position, that in any given election the party or candidate who is perceived as moderate or centrist competing against an ideologist of the left or right is in a better position. Consequently, when one party nominates someone who is seen as being on the extreme of his party while the other party selects a nominee who seems to be a moderate, the latter usually wins, often overwhelmingly. In 1964, when Senator Goldwater was perceived as a right-winger running against a Southern moderate Democrat, he was trounced in a 60-40 election. Conversely, Senator McGovern, seen as equally ideological on the other side, was beaten even worse in 1972. When both nominees are seen as moderates, as in 1976, we have a relatively close contest.

Given the way our political process operates, while it would seem likely that center candidates would dominate (as they did in the 1976 situation), it is possible to envisage a situation with a Goldwater and a McGovern running in the same election. Since the college educated and the ideologists, groups that overlap considerably, are much more active politically than the moderates and centrists, the former may increase their influence and control over party nominations at all levels as they grow in numbers. Such a development, of course, would create a fundamentally new kind of party system in America.

Meanwhile, it should be noted that the Democrats are more likely to come up with moderate or centrist candidates while the Republicans pick ideologists or conservatives. Since Democrats outnumber registered Republicans by close to two-to-one, this means that the Democrats include more moderates than the GOP. As the Republicans have lost support, what remains of the party is inherently more ideological. The largest faction in the Democratic party is composed of predominantly working-class and white ethnic people (overlapping categories) who tend to be economic liberals and social or cultural conservatives, i.e., Meany Democrats. A smaller percentage of this segment votes in primaries in comparison with the better-educated, more affluent, consistent liberals espousing the New Politics, yet their base is so much larger that they can still determine the results of primaries. In 1976, for example, Jackson and Carter, the moderate candidates, did much better than Udall, Harris, and other more liberal candidates in the running for the presidential nomination. Within the GOP, however, Reagan did much better than anticipated against an incumbent, and Ford moved considerably to the right in order to beat him for the nomination, a fact that hurt him in the contest with Carter.

HOROWITZ Another way of examining the electoral process is to treat presidential politics as a game in which a series of wild cards are played. Certainly, specific choices of candidates cannot be reduced to a triadic system based upon conservative, liberal, or radical options. A range of issue orientations are involved in electoral politics that are at least as important as functional prerequisites of office holders. The phenomenology of national politics in this country has become most complex.

Political scientists often talk about political life as if it were a rational phenomenon, as if tendencies worked their way out inexorably in terms of historical preferences and philosophies. But that is not what has taken place. The assassination of John F. Kennedy in 1963 changed the relationship between regional and sectional forces; it gave America a southwestern President, Lyndon Baines Johnson. This period was marked by an imperial presidency in which the role of commander in chief became dominant, even though Johnson's domestic political programs were the most liberal yet proposed in the history of the United States. Johnson possessed a sincere liberal imagination on questions ranging from rent control and rat control to urban development. But he performed poorly as commander in chief in relation to Vietnam. This performance, not his successful liberal or left-of-center formulas, cost him renomination.

The election campaign of 1968 witnessed the assassination of Robert F. Kennedy. This special event, which eliminated the front-running Democratic candidate, created a climate that made possible, in some measure, the election of Richard M. Nixon. The Republican victory might not have taken place had there been a Kennedy-Nixon face-off. Hubert H. Humphrey did very well in the electoral campaign, surprisingly well, judging from pre-election polls. The interruption of a so-called normal electoral process is far different from the kind of Weberian rationality guiding much analysis. One might argue that such personal catastrophes do not disrupt the political process per se, only the actors in that process. But I view such a democratic determinism as dangerously optimistic and ultimately negating the role of the individual in American history.

Beyond politicals as accidental, there is also politics as symbolic. The electoral process may be significant primarily as an expression of general ideological inclinations. There can be no doubt that the actual leverage of a president is limited by a wide variety of constraints that are budgetary no less than political. For example, at the budgetary level there is an interesting contrast between reality and rhetoric. Under the Nixon-Ford administrations, one would have anticipated a decline in the amount of funds siphoned off from welfare and social benefit programs. But that is not the case. Quite the contrary. The inexorable tendency of the Republican party, no less than the Democratic party, has been to insure that a necessary portion of the Gross National Product went to satisfy the needs of the underclass: to ensure that the underclass would not employ violence against other members of society; to insure that it would remain stable, steady, and essentially nonviolent. So whether the rationale was fear of violence or a belief in social welfare as such, the actual differences between the parties on such vital subjects have been relatively minimal in contrast to the rhetoric that separates the two parties on these issues.

While there are different mixes between funds provided for one social science in contrast to another, or applied research in contrast to pure research, the Republicans, during their administrative reign, have given as much money to these areas as the Democrats before or since. Again, whatever the rationale—a belief in the role of science, or a fear of intellectual backlash—the gap between the party system is much smaller in reality than in rhetoric. What one often finds as the level of presidential politics are thus symbols or shadows lacking in substance. It is not so certain that politics resides in the presidential office as it is that whichever party holds the office affects a symbolic identification of the office with a particular ideology. In fact, there is usually little to differentiate the candidates, if for no other reason than the fact that fiscal programming and budgeting involve years of advance preparation. The consequence of this is that presidential politics is often leaning in one direction rather than another. In this way, a president can be instrumental in setting the tone for national sentiments on questions of a concrete variety from school desegregation to teenage abortion.

One important point made by people like Eli Ginzberg and Sar Levitan is that the programs of the 1960s, despite the fact that they were often criticized and reviled, were in fact largely successful in their aims. They created a climate of relative political tranquility by responding to a widely held consensus that every American has a right to the basic protections of shelter, food, and clothing. By shifting the burdens from individuals to governments, the state at once became more powerful and individuals felt more tranquil because someone was out there listening to their complaints. No presidential candidate would dare interrupt this process of welfare beyond some modest cosmetics to make the programs operate more effectively and efficiently or to weed out corruption in its more obvious forms, or he would risk either a revolution or a counterrevolution. Even a candidate like Ronald Reagan only marginally interfered with the welfare system while governor of California. All this again points out that presidential politics involves an array of considerations extending far beyond conventional political labels.

We now have a bureaucratic establishment so large and so autonomous that it tends to perform its tasks almost without regard to which party occupies the presidential Oval Office. Demands for trimming the size or the budget of the bureaucracy are made frequently, but there are so many exemptions from such demands and so many constraints on either executive or legislative action that the bureaucratic structure conducts its affairs almost without regard to the occupant of the White House. In times of greatest crisis, as, for example, during the Watergate period, an autonomous middle-management bureaucratic structure provided continuity and stability even though the elites themselves were under extraordinary pressure, and even disarray.

The policy apparatus in the United States is probably closer to the Platonic ideal than to that of any others we have seen since ancient Athens. It operates in terms of an interchangeability of elites with respect to how they function, the roles they assume, and the tasks they perform. These bureaucratic elites operate largely without party affiliation, or, at most, with minimal party affiliation. Apart from the several thousand top cadres that any incumbent

President has the right to appoint, there is little interruption in the political process as a result of elections. It is important for a variety of reasons to make this point as clearly and as concretely as possible: first, we should not take presidential politics too seriously; second, we should not assume that the operations of government are beholden to the electoral processes except in relatively marginal ways.

This is a sensitive issue. The president does indeed have power, and even bureaucracies are not oblivious to that power. But the entire range of administrative detail, middle-management procedures, and bureaucratic operations have their own inexorable laws that probably affect presidential behavior no less than presidential incumbents affect administrative bureaucratic behavior.

LIPSET   There is no question that you are right in stressing the extent to which elections result in changes in the presidency but do not bring about fundamental changes. If you consider the presidency of Eisenhower, which seemingly was designed to reverse the New Deal programs of Roosevelt and Truman, and that of Nixon, which promised to counter the Great Society programs of Kennedy and Johnson, they did not change trends much. Under Nixon and Ford, the size of the book containing government regulations tripled from 20,000 to 60,000 pages.

The differences between democratic parties in postindustrial societies suggest that they should vary with respect to efforts to modify the existing distribution of privilege while in office. In fact, conservative governments rarely try to curtail programs previously enacted to improve the lot of the underprivileged. The Labor party brought in an extensive program of socialized medicine in Britain. The Conservatives opposed it, but when the Tories were elected, all they did was to tinker with the system, essentially to put on a show. Instead of having free drugs they charged a shilling. Basically they did not modify the socialized medical system. Labor nationalized some industries; the Tories came back and denationalized the trucking industry, but fundamentally they did not make major changes. The same thing has been true in the United States, although the Democrats have not enacted the kind of dramatic legislation that Labor did when they first came into power in Britain. The American conservatives, that is, the Republicans, like the Conservatives in England and elsewhere, have opposed major social reforms, but when they return to office they find that most reforms have been institutionalized—they have acquired a kind of vested interest of their own. In effect, all the conservatives can do is try and make them work better—to be more efficient.

The logic of budget expansion operates under conservatives as under liberals. Under the supposedly business-oriented Nixon administration, the National Endowment for the Arts and the National Endowment for the Humanities, two government foundations that give money to support art, culture, humanistic, and, to some extent, social science studies, had their budgets quadrupled, from $20 to $80 million a year each. You would think that the Republican party, the hard-headed party, would oppose these institutions, particularly since they were initiated under Democrats. The constituency of the Republican party includes few intellectuals, academics, artists, or theatre people. Yet the Republican party, a Republican president, proposed these dramatic increases. The Democratic Congress did not force them into such a cultural posture.

There are, of course, major differences in the central core of the two rival coalitions. As Charles Beard noted before World War I, the average Democratic voter is somewhat less privileged than the average Republican. The lower-status ethnic and religious groups—those of more recent immigrant status, those distant in ancestral background from Anglo-Saxon and northern European Protestants—are more disposed to back the Democrats. Since the Democrats have been the party of the less privileged in economic and status terms, the party is identified with efforts to modify the stratification system, to foster greater equality. The Republicans do not defend inequality; rather, they emphasize liberty. They view increased government power as threatening to liberty and usually as incompetent to remedy the social evils its expansion is designed to accomplish.

There are differences in practice. The Ford administration tried to do away with some regulatory agencies, to open up more free competition. These proposals, however, were usually resisted by the businesses involved. As Republican opponents of regulation pointed out, many regulatory agencies reduce risks and create the functional equivalent of monopolies. Until recently, few Democrats have worried about the growing power of the state. They have favored leaning on the state to solve social problems and to do away with poverty. But the constraints of power affect them as well. Concern with the costs of government and an awareness that many of the welfare programs have failed have led Democrats from Massachusetts (Governor Dukakis) to California (Governor Jerry Brown) to act like fiscal conservatives. They have cut back on welfare assistance and medical programs, and have shifted priorities in education from elite higher education to mass education. In part they are responding to a taxpayers' revolt produced by the inflationary cycle. The recession of the 1970s has meant less revenue for the states. The situation that New York City and New York state face exists to a lesser, but similar extent in many other states and cities. These events have reduced the number of differences between the parties on the state level as well.

In California, for example, Ronald Reagan increased the budget sharply during his term as governor. He argues that the increase is less striking than it appears since part of the increase was simply an accounting change: the state took over responsibility for raising revenues previously collected on the local level, which were then reapportioned to the schools and other agencies. The fact remains that the California state budget increased considerably under Ronald Reagan. Conversely, under Governor Brown the rate of budget growth has been curtailed largely, I believe, because he took office in a period of economic decline. Economic conditions proved to be more important than ideology, more important also than the constraints imposed by varying constituencies. We ought to turn now to a different, but related concern: the role of the intelligentsia.

Many scholars and other people, including both of us, have taken cognizance of the rise of what has been called the new intelligentsia—a large, politically relevant stratum composed mainly of college-educated people, meaning not just intellectuals and academics but professionals, technicians, scientists, people in journalism and the media, and the like. This awareness emerges in the context of projecting the future of politics in advanced industrial democratic societies, and this group, which now forms a sizeable proportion of the population, plays a major role in setting the agenda for society. They are the people who create new ideas and propagate them to the public through television, printed journalism, and other media. In the United States, as well as other countries, they have tended to be on the left politically. They form the core of the McGovern New Politics faction here. Similar groups exist in most European countries, where they tend to be in the more activist wings of the socialist or labor parties.

This group of educated, affluent leftists is highly critical of the values and institutions of existing Western societies, considering the noncommunist, nonsocialist countries as too materialistic, corrupt, and bureaucratic. They hold up as a goal a kind of postmaterialistic world in which government is concerned with the problems of ecology and clean environment. The intelligentsia are also egalitarians, particularly with respect to women's liberation, minority racial groups, and related causes. They are less interested, however, in the working class. It must be admitted that since the end of the Vietnam war the intelligentsia seem to be less effective as a political force than they once appeared to be. But they remain a major force. One of the most interesting questions concerning the future of American politics is what role they will play in determining new agendas and new issues in post-industrial America.

HOROWITZ   The extent to which an expanded intelligentsia has come to form the base of a new class is rapidly becoming a major issue unto itself. The difficulty with Lipset's position is that one ends up with an intelligentsia that is uniquely comprised of technicians, and, by virtue of that, presumably a new class that embodies scientific objectivity. Yet, while there can be no question that intellectuals as a class have become more central to the policymaking apparatus, it is far less certain that such an apparatus is itself lacking an ideology or profound biases. All classes come into existence preaching their universality and end up displaying their intense particularity.

I would now like to harken back to the points Lipset raised concerning the current division between equality and liberty, and how that division has profoundly affected political party postures. There is, for example, no doubt that the party of equality is the Democratic party and that the party of liberty is the Republican party. What is in doubt is whether either concept separated from the other is anything more than an ideological whipping-post calculated to make various constituencies pleased with the political processes. There is a somewhat different mapping of the problem of equality versus liberty that might be drawn.

If one reexamines the nineteenth century, especially the European experiments with benign monarchy, one notes that countries such as Germany, France, and Russia were characterized by a structure in which the fundamental truths of society were embodied in the state. The Hegelian vision, whether of a right-wing or left-wing variety, holds that the power of the state is more binding and worthy than the power of class, and certainly more potent than that of international organization. But this emphasis on state power and the centrality of the nation has also led to a vision of individuals as beholden to state and nation, and, furthermore, to a view of those organizations that demand equality as divisive, as trying to eat away at the legitimate power of the state. That is why European societies still tend to be more conservative than American society. When demands for equality could not be suppressed, they resulted in sharp class confrontations and revolutions, such as those that took place in France, Germany, and Russia.

The United States, almost from the outset, tended to promote the idea of equality of opportunity, if not of function.

As a result, individualism led to a belief not only in the worth of persons, but in the superiority of their claims over and against the claims of the state. Hence, as everyone from John Jay to Hannah Arendt understood, the United States has been a compassionate rather than a passionate nation. It is presumed that everyone has a right to live, to survive, and to enjoy a certain amount of dignity by virtue of his humanity. It was these sentiments, embodied in the first ten amendments to the Constitution, that really distinguished American egalitarianism from European libertarianism.

The ontological core of this new persuasion is that people no longer had to be overwhelmed with the guilt that inheres to the question: "Where have I failed?" Rather, they had the right, even the mandate, to ask: "Where has the political system failed me?" Of course, all forms of psychological reductionism carry penalties, and the claim that the state alone is at fault—that only the state has lacked in provisions—leads to the sort of exaggeration that is almost inevitable within an egalitarian frame of reference. But the fact does remain that any electoral process must take seriously this shift from European libertarianism to American egalitarianism. No party that hopes to succeed in the United States can ignore the egalitarian passion and the democratic temper that describe the American people.

Specifically, answers to questions about the obligations of the state and the rights of citizens can over time become answers to questions about personal failure. Why have we not risen on the mobility ladder? Why have we not gotten the commodities we desire? Increasingly, the answer played back is that the state, the nation, the system—however one wants to characterize mechanisms of rule—are at fault. It is the constancy of demand on the system or, conversely, the unwillingness of the individual to accept the idea that there

are limits to personal growth and development that makes
the present moment in American history so volatile. It is not
the crumbling of party identification or political preferences, or even alienation or anomie, that ultimately is the
root issue. For each of these can somehow be accommodated
by new political parties or new forms of social integration.
But given the wholehearted commitment of Americans to a
functionalist rather than an organic view, to a view in
which the citizen sees no compromise with the absolute that
the state is beholden to its citizenry and that in no sense are
citizens beholden to the state, disintegrating norms must be
expected. Clearly, today the potential for reconciliation is
small. Unless we, as citizens, recognize that no society can
provide all its people all the time with all their wants, civil
strife becomes just about inevitable.

LIPSET   That is a good point. The Tri-Lateral Commission—Europe, America, and Japan—has been issuing a series of reports on problems faced by these societies. Recent
monographs on politics—both the American report, written by Sam Huntington of Harvard, and the European
one, written by Michel Crozier of Paris—discuss the same
point you make. That is, the demands on the system have
become so great that the state cannot accommodate them,
cannot simultaneously give different activist groups what
they want because their demands are often contradictory.

To turn to a related point, it is necessary to recognize
that, historically, American radicalism, utopianism, has
been antistatist and individualistic. The American national
self-image emerged in a revolt against the centralized European monarchial state; on one hand, it has emphasized
equality, and, on the other, it has been antistatist. Our labor

movement has been syndicalist, antistatist, both in its more moderate AFL form and in its revolutionary IWW variety. The European labor movements, by contrast, have demanded that the state do things for them. Until the 1930s, both the radical and moderate American union movements said, "We do not want state help. We want to improve the lot of workers ourself; we do not trust the state."

The Jeffersonian tradition, the fount of our liberal-left tradition, is an antistatist one. In analyzing why socialist movements have not succeeded in this country, some have related the failure to the nature of America's antistatist, anticollectivist, individualistic value systems. This, as Professor Horowitz has suggested, has clearly changed, starting with the changes that occurred in the New Deal period as a reaction to the depression. One may even date the emergence of an American welfare orientation back to the Progressive movement prior to World War I. A famous Russian scholar, Moise Ostrogorski, who was in the U.S. in the 1890s, wrote what is considered to be one of the classic books on American politics, *Democracy and the Organization of Political Parties*. Ostrogorski concluded that the United States was on an inevitable road to socialism, since its Congress had voted that groups needing economic assistance from the state could have it. The law Ostrogorski was referring to is the McKinley Tariff, passed by the Republicans. Ostrogorski was convinced that business had set the U.S. on the road to socialism by pressing the government to support the interests of one class against another. His was a highly rationalistic assumption; politics obviously are not that rational. State intervention, he argued, once accepted, clearly would become linked to the credo of equality, a credo that goes back to the Revolution and the Declaration of Independence and that emphasizes equality of respect and equality of opportunity.

Considerations of equality require that we face up to the implications of the generalization made by the great commentator on American society, Alexis de Tocqueville. Tocqueville observed that once the idea of equality came into the world it was unbeatable. The idea that all people, especially the poor and underprivileged, should be guaranteed equality is one that cannot be challenged on a moral basis. This generalization goes far toward explaining the strength of the left in many western countries. Various social scientists and economists have made the case for inequality of reward by contending that a society characterized by division of labor—with different occupational positions that require differential levels of education, skills, and the like—must reward people unequally. They hold that some degree of inequality of reward is necessary in order to motivate people to go to school for many years so they may successfully do the kinds of things necessary to carry out such roles as physician, scholar, businessman, political leader—roles that require high levels of intelligence, diligence, long hours of work, and an ability to endure prolonged states of tension or anxiety about outcomes.

At the same time, it is morally difficult to justify inequality of reward linked to accidents of birth. I am not just talking about suffering for being born black or poor. What about the ugly or the dull-witted? Should they be punished for these defects? Punishment is, in fact, what differential rewards involve. The lowly are negatively regarded, and that is painful. Equality of opportunity does not justify inequality of result, for if people start the race unequally, then equality of opportunity does not exist.

Inequality, severe stratification, is no longer morally acceptable. Hence, the privileged within nations and those living in wealthier societies are faced with the fact that the advantages they have are no longer legitimate. This is true even though the highly advantaged, even the left-wingers among them, do not relinquish their wealth. Senator Edward Kennedy has frequently written letters to the *New York Times,* taking extreme egalitarian positions. Is the fact that one does not read of the Kennedys or of other wealthy egalitarians giving up any of their wealth evidence of hypocrisy, proof that the words are empty? I would say no. Few give up their advantages willingly, even if they no longer believe in their right to have them. But once the legitimacy of a claim to superiority is undermined, once there no longer is a moral basis for privilege, those who have wealth and status are defeated in the long-term struggle.

This is the point Tocqueville made well over 150 years ago. This is what gives egalitarian movements, or rather those that have claimed to be (I should emphasize that most egalitarian movements really do not foster equality when they come to power), such a tremendous advantage. The main reason the Democratic party is currently the majority party in this country is that it is seen as the party of equality. The Republican party is perceived as the party of business. It is the party of the well-to-do, and most people, including many of the wealthy and especially their college-educated offspring, who benefit from unearned wealth do not want to be identified with defending privilege.

HOROWITZ The fly in the ointment of the Huntington solution* and that of my colleague (who participated in the special issue of *The Public Interest* about America at 200

---

*Samuel P. Huntington, "The Democratic Distemper," *The Public Interest,* no. 41 (Fall 1975), pp. 9–38; Seymour Martin Lipset, "The Paradox of American Politics," *ibid.,* pp. 142–165.

years) is not so much the problem of the democratic distemper (although that is an arguable premise unto itself). Rather, it is the political necessity of inequality that underwrites this entire approach. The argument essentially states that the democratic rage is too costly in economic terms, and too menacing in political terms, and hence for the purpose of system maintenance, certain curbs, or at least limits on democracy, are inevitable.

It serves little purpose to keep harking back to the writing of Alexis de Tocqueville in order to glean the essential truths of late-twentieth-century America. There is no gainsaying the remarkable insights Tocqueville had about pre-Civil War America, and, beyond that, his observations of manners and mores of Americans that have indeed persisted over time. But to use this kind of approach to state an ideological position, namely, that democracy is too expensive and fragile to endure in more than a handful of nations throughout the world and, further, that the price of continuing to move along on a democratic axis may be too high, seems to me a misuse of history. It is more important to come to terms with changes in the American situation: the rise of militarism and multinationalism, for example, both of which profoundly affect the character of American manners and mores. If democracy becomes fragile in America, it is less a function of the cost of maintaining such a system than of the impossibility of maintaining such a system internally while engaging in colonial warfare abroad.

The military factor, rather than traditional political factors, is the missing piece in the conventional, functional interpretations. As a result, questions of equality are cast in a framework of economic costs rather than military liabilities. Obviously, one can no longer expect adherence to an old-fashioned, neo-Darwinian, organic view that inequality is somehow moral and stimulates social health. Even the most conservative of us have moved beyond the idea of a struggle to survive as a basis of moral fitness or, concomitantly, beyond the idea that those who fail to survive under such a struggle for existence somehow deserve to perish. As I have said before, the idea of competition, while potent in American life, never took such powerful roots as it did in European civilization.

The great genius of American civilization is that it came with civility. In America the struggle to survive and the need for economic and social competition involved in nation building was made less harsh by the state's interest in assisting those individuals not capable of making it on their own. It was in America that the notion of political compassion was first introduced, and it was this political compassion that probably spared America the worst infirmities of European revolutions and counterrevolutions. Professor Lipset is correct, of course, that once utilitarians made their argument in favor of equality there was no longer any question of where the tilt was, namely, on the team believing in equality and not on the side of those who presumably believed in liberty. But such an abstraction, polarization, and reification of concepts minimizes the impact of a growing global militarism, of which the United States is very much a part. Even if one can successfully argue the necessity of such militarism and arms buildup, the consequences for the concepts of equity and liberty alike seem to pale in importance.

This underscores one difficulty in Professor Lipset's approach: an assumption that the political process is an autonomous series of events and, likewise, that economic processes are also relatively autonomous. While his analysis provides great sophistication at these levels, post-Tocquevillian elements such as militarism and multinationalism simply have no place in his analysis. The American nation becomes, in this analysis, a self-contained unit, a kind of approach far easier to maintain in 1945 when, as a consequence of World War II, American world hegemony was complete than it is in 1977 when that hegemony has been considerably eroded. This transformation of America from leader of the world empire to an important player in world events accounts for much current handwringing about the future of democracy in a completely hegemonic world. Of course, for the rest of civilization this is clearly too high a price to pay.

The progression, the evolution of the Harvard school of political economy and political sociology, is precisely the move from the idea of the United States as the first new nation and the world's leading democratic state, as exemplified in Lipset's work, to a less benign view of the United States. The U.S. is first among many notions in the world economic struggle linked to the multinational corporate system. It is also first or second, depending on how one views Soviet military might, in the area of armed forces and military hardware, no less than technology generally. Hence, the evolution of that Harvard position has been from an utter disregard of the military and international pivots, which do make America strong, to a belief that only these pivots could keep America strong in the future. The analysis of the military factor is absent in the work of Lipset and very much present in the work of Huntington and others. Yet both have a shared confidence in the hidden boot of American foreign policy. The inhibitions to political democracy are seen in terms of the need to maintain national security. The minute we begin talking about this dimension of American political life, problems spoken of earlier such as regional, coalitional, and sectoral politics, or left, center, and right formations in a political ideology, must be viewed as a rather modest aspect of the ongoing debate as to the nature of the American political process.

LIPSET   Here is a basic disagreement. If you look at the role of the military in terms of the percentage it receives of the Gross National Product, it is evident that support has been declining steadily in the United States since the Korean War with a temporary interruption posed by Vietnam. The two biggest departments of the federal government are the Pentagon (the Department of Defense) and the Department of Health, Education, and Welfare. HEW is now much the larger department. The American military is much weaker now than it has been at any time since World War II. An ironic and amazing fact is that in replacing the weaponry and ammunition used up by Israel during the course of the Yom Kippur War, the United States came close to stripping itself of conventional weaponry. The United States actually sent a considerable portion of its conventional weaponry to tiny Israel. That support used up the American military arsenal.

This notion that the military is a drain on the productive resources of the developed Western countries is simply not true. It is the poorer Third World and communist nations that, in seeking to maintain modern military establishments, spend large proportions of the Gross National Product (GNP) for war. Unfortunately, a number of these less developed countries, for reasons often linked to the aggressiveness of relations with their neighbors, have inhibited their own individual development by emphasizing defense. Placed in a worldwide context, the equality debate is not a matter of responding to people defending inequality, but rather of reacting to questions of human liberty and state power. That is, it deals with the argument that increases in the power of the bureaucratic state designed to facilitate social and economic egalitarian policies result in threats to liberty and democracy, thereby restricting human rights.

In the United States we now have an interesting phenomenon. Groups on the ideological left and right argue that democracy has been weakened. On one end, there is Milton Friedman, who stands for complete laissez-faire as a kind of conservative anarchist (or, if you will, libertarian, to use a phrase preferred by many people who hold positions like his). He argues that the increase in state control, state intervention in the economy, inevitably has decreased liberty—that we have much less liberty in the United States now than in earlier years. On the other hand, various political leftists have argued the same point, identifying the growth of the military-industrial complex as the key element that has reduced individual freedom. They are both wrong. The elaboration of First Amendment rights by the Supreme Court, as well as the challenges to executive power by a newly strengthened Congress have enhanced liberty. The rights, for example, of the accused are better protected today than they have ever been. Journalists have more freedom from employer, advertiser, or government dictates. There are more contested elections and a greater turnover of officials in trade unions than I can ever recall.

We have just gone through a war (the Vietnam war) where the opponents of the war had more rights than radical and/or antiwar groups ever had in wartime in any country I have ever heard about (even with all the attempts made by the government to repress dissent—attempts properly exposed by the Congress). During the Civil War habeas corpus was suspended by Lincoln. During World War I the government put many opponents of the war in jail, and after the war foreign-born opponents of the war were deported. The Korean War saw the rise of McCarthyism. During the Vietnam war, college students who were antiwar, representing campus newspapers, were flown around Vietnam by the U.S. Army. The antistatist tradition in the United States, institutionalized in First Amendment rights and other constitutional protections, has meant greater freedom of speech and protest here than in other democracies, which we think of as free societies, such as France, Great Britain, and Canada. Many of the rights we take for granted simply do not exist in these countries.

For example, the newspapers in the United States become terribly excited whenever a court suggests that a paper should not print certain stories about people accused of crimes until the trial is over. They insist that restrictions on pretrial publicity are a violation of basic freedoms, and they almost invariably win their cases. In Britain, once a person is arrested, the newspaper may not print a story about that person. When Daniel Ellsberg took the Pentagon Papers, it turned out there was no law under which he could be indicted other than stealing. He was indicted for stealing paper, i.e., government property. The British have an Official Secrets Act, which provides that if a civil servant reveals a government secret, he can go to prison for twenty years or more. The United States does not have a comparable law. An attempt to sneak an Official Secrets Act into a Senate bill revising the criminal code aroused the outrage of many people, and it did not pass. The democratic rights of the individual, whether to express himself politically or defend himself in a criminal case, are probably in better shape than ever before.

There is another serious question raised by Professor Horowitz as to whether our election mechanism still is significant given the tremendous growth of the bureaucratic state. Is it possible for elections to result in fundamental changes? That is another issue. As I noted earlier, the bigger the state, the more bureaucratic control the state has, the greater the continuity from one administration to another. To reiterate, it probably makes less difference now than in the past whether we elect a Democratic or a Republican president since the country is so heavily committed to massive costly policies that cannot be reversed easily.

But again, consider what has happened in this country in just one decade. I am quite willing to confess that if somebody in 1965 told me that ten years in the future—or, more accurately, in but five years from then—there would be the kind of changes with respect to the rights of homosexuals, the position and status of women, the position and rights of blacks, the legal rights of the accused, and the growth of "sexual permissiveness" that have occurred in the United States, I would have told them they were crazy. Such massive social changes do not occur that fast. These changes occurred in large part as a result of social movements and protest activity. Dynamic reform processes did continue, and these developed, interestingly enough, outside the party system, outside the electoral system. It was not the election of particular candidates that affected the position of homosexuals or modified the status of women. The major change that occurred was in the larger conscience of people, a change in values, in conceptions of what is proper and what is right. These came about in part because some people went out and put their bodies on the line. They protested, got involved, made it evident that as members of minority groups they felt morally offended at the way they were treated. And the society reacted—often grudgingly, often in ways that a majority would have rejected in a referendum as Miami did—but change they did.

One of the things that puzzles me is the role played by the courts in these processes. The courts in the United States have obviously played a major role in effecting social change—in giving expression to new concepts of right and wrong, morality, as well as the individual citizen's rights. They seemingly have responded to larger changes in the larger body politic and in particular to the increased influence of the intelligentsia discussed earlier. But why judges and lawyers, who have been thought largely of as part of the privileged, relatively conservative establishment, should play this kind of dynamic role is a phenomenon I confess I do not really understand. It is true that ideally the law is supposed to be universalistic, that it operates on the assumption of no favoritism shown toward any one group.

From this it may be deduced that what the courts have been doing has been to give expression to universalistic, egalitarian norms and morality. But why have they so consistently backed reform—from the one man-one vote decision to those decisions dealing with the rights of blacks, abortion, and extensions of the rights of women and old people? These changes suggest a great extension of the forces for equality that also have enhanced the freedom of various groups at the same time that the increased power of the bureaucracy and the regulatory agencies has enhanced the power of the state over the individual.

HOROWITZ   So many points have been introduced by Professor Lipset in his latest remarks that it is difficult to avoid a direct reply. I will therefore risk becoming involved in a syndrome of challenge and response, at least on several matters of fact.

It is true that there has been a considerable plateauing of the military budget. But the United States began this leveling off from a position of having either the first or second largest allocation for military affairs in the entire world. Beyond that, while certain marginal reductions in the size of the United States' armed forces are possible, and will in all likelihood take place, the cost factor is generally inflexible. This is due to the nature of a technological military, namely, its reliance on nuclear components rather than conventional armaments. As the United States moves from a labor-intensive to a capital-intensive military, that is, from a military based on sheer numbers to one based on technological potential, those cost factors will become even more rigorously defined. That is why the SALT I and SALT II negotiations necessarily emphasize not the reduction in manpower but rather limits upon new forms of military technology. Only in this way can a durable, long-term reduction in military expenditures be achieved. This is a matter of joint international rationality rather than American will or desire. A good indication of this is the inability of the United States to move the Soviet Union toward a mutual withdrawal pact for all of Europe. As a result these talks remain in limbo.

The impact of militarism can not be calculated simply by totaling budgetary expenditures on the armed forces. Rather, the consequences of a permanent military establishment of enormous size and position must be considered. Indeed, Kenneth Boulding, among others, has referred to a permanent World War III syndrome in which the United States, since its initial mobilization in 1939, has resisted a large-scale standing army of several million, relying instead on large-scale technological expenditures in the area of military and nuclear deterrents. This overall militarization not only affects foreign affairs but domestic life as well. It provides the national system with swollen police forces, paramilitary groups, vigilante societies, civil defense organizations, surveillance fetishes, and a host of other human and physical properties that are directly linked to the utilization of large-scale military systems to achieve political tranquility.

It would seem to be a profound error to claim that a reduction in the size of the Department of Defense by 2 or 3 percent necessarily indicates a great victory for the Department of Health, Education, and Welfare. A diminution in the budget of one agency does not necessarily signify an increment to that of another. For example, the cuts in the DoD have been largely administrative, whereas hardware commitments have actually increased over time. Such thinking fails to reckon with the impact of foreign military adventures on the domestic scene. The question of militarism, in our time at least, involves the issue of military failure. In terms of simply winning and losing games, World War II was a winning game, the Korean War a stalemate, and the Vietnam war a losing one.

The military has lost in stature as it has grown in size. As its overseas activities have been weakened, its domestic potential has been strengthened. A particularly dangerous fact is that the military, despite its size, carries no real popular consensus. Stalemates and losses sap the military of a public morale, and hence lead to sharp differentiation of the military from the civilian population. Every American president has had to fact that fact. And some, like President Lyndon Johnson, have had to resign in the face of such a fact.

To say that out of the Vietnam war experience there came a growth in civil liberties or to assume a parallel between growing international warfare and growing domestic equality is naive. Neither possibility treats seriously the ambiguous character of that war, not to mention the ongoing demands of minorities and largely excluded groups from participation in the society. (This last has nothing to do with the war, except, of course, to use antiwar sentiment as a mechanism for mobilizing other forms of domestic-political struggle.)

Recourse to a term like ambiguity may reflect weakness or blockage on the part of the analyst, but I think not. I suspect that the American present is characterized by a series of ambiguities. What constitutes a war and what does not? What constitutes civil rights in contrast to civic obligations? What constitutes racial equality? How many individuals can participate in this egalitarianism? Simple participation in the American political system, as a recipient of its benefits, may not be enough. Interest group identities—alliances of class, women, youth, or what have you—may turn out to be a crucial aspect that could make any real future identification with the American polity as a whole extremely difficult. There are many ways societies fall apart even as they satisfy great numbers of wants and needs.

There is another dimension to the question of civil liberties in the American scene, namely, the selective nature of such pursuits. The nation has taken a tolerant and expansive view where the rights of homosexuals and deviant groups such as drug addicts and alcoholics are involved, but when political innovation or experimentation is at issue, it has taken a much more restrictive posture. We are at a period in American life when it is far easier to be socially deviant than politically marginal. The range of options in deviant behavior is nearly infinite at the very time when the range of political options has been reduced to such a degree that even the formation of a third party is an anachronistic thought.

Another way of viewing the same problem is to say the flowering of the private life has come at the expense of the public one. In an odd way, liberation from gender roles and prescribed behavior, in the very act of enhancing the private life, has not had a corresponding spillover in political liberation. There has been, in fact, a diminished interest by those who formerly committed themselves to working in the public sphere for the common good. This is vouchsafed by decreasing political alignments, decreasing political participation, and decreasing public belief that such participation will have any long-range consequences. The very intelligentsia that is presumably a weathervane of public affairs has been one of the first to opt out of public life in favor of a more private existence. Further, as public troubles mount, their resolution is viewed by these former activists in terms of further increasing privatization. The turn to psychology on the part of the intelligentsia has led to the search for personal fulfillment and individual satisfaction not only as the instrument of a happy life but as the goal of that life as well. such intense psychologism most benefits those currently in power. By granting the citizenry a sense of personal freedom, those in control of government risk little to their own survival and security.

To argue that civil liberties is simply concerned with the enhancement of the private life is to miss a large chunk of what has taken place in America. The enhancement of the private life has been acquired in an unspoken quid pro quo, that is, at the expense of public forms of protest. More significantly, participation in public affairs has become eccentric. Cynicism has emerged as a widespread response to all forms of public information and public services. Such cynicism is not a function of repression, but a belief that only private, immediate gratification is genuine. For that reason, I would suggest that Professor Lipset's belief that the past decade has seen a flowering of American civil liberties is not based on a reasoned evaluation of the whole picture.

Impressive gains *have* been made in the rights of Americans in the private sector, and these gains *are* real and have served to remind us of the potency of the Bill of Rights. But it would seem to me entirely myopic not to recognize that these private sector gains have been traded off at a cost of serious erosion in the performance of the public sector. As a result, it is premature to celebrate an increase in civil liberties, especially at a time of a decrease in civil rights.

LIPSET   I disagree with a number of points you made, but unfortunately our time is running out. I would just say in passing that I do not quite recognize the same world, live in the same America in the last few years that you do. The period from 1965 through the early 1970s was one in which the greatest participation in protest activities occurred—more than ever before in American history, certainly in modern American history. While there has been a decline from the Vietnam protest period, there is still a massive active women's liberation movement, and many citizen groups are active in the ecology area, which have constituted themselves almost as veto groups in decisions concerning highways, new building, anything that may affect the environment and the like. But these are matters we can perhaps get into later. At this point we should allow the panel of people who are prepared to ask questions to take part in our discussion.

QUESTION   We have heard a lot of noise about this new thing called neo-conservatism. I have yet to hear a good definition of it. Perhaps you gentlemen could define it, and I would be curious to know if you think it is anything more than a short-lived phenomenon?

LIPSET   The best definition I have seen of neo-conservatism appeared in an article in *Newsweek,* by Irving Kristol, who is the leader, insofar as one can talk of such a tendency. In this article Kristol wrote that neo-conservatives are people who are concerned about threats to liberty that have come about from the increase in state power. In the present context of American and world politics, they see this increase in state and bureaucratic power and the various negative consequences of it as phenomena that greatly need resistance, exposure, and analysis. But they still differ from plain conservatives, or old-fashioned conservatives, since most of the "neo's" believe in many of the values of the liberal left tradition from which they stem.

The neo-conservatives still believe in welfare objectives, in increased equality. Kristol emphasized that in another context, in another period, if the problems that now concern him were ever resolved, he might once more take his place as a liberal seeking the extension of welfare objectives. Those dubbed "neo-conservative" are then a group of people who were once actively involved in liberal or radical left politics and who, while not abandoning their concerns for equality, feel that the current political scene has interposed other threats to freedom and equality. These threats particularly arise out of the growth of bureaucratic state power and the expansion of communism internationally, both of which need to be resisted. A neoconservative believes that the experiences of the past four decades indicate that the standard liberal solutions to problems—increasing government involvement, regulation, and expenditures—have frequently created more problems than they've solved.

They are concerned, therefore, with what Robert Merton has called the "unanticipated consequences of purposeful social change." As some see it (they are not all of one mind), many of the social changes of the past few decades, which were designed to extend equality and to upgrade the bottom, like the welfare programs, have brought with them unanticipated destructive consequences for the individuals who were supposed to be helped. In this context, for example, *The Public Interest,* which is edited by Kristol, has carried a number of interesting articles by Tom Sowell. Sowell, a black economist, has pointed out that one of the consequences of the pressure for school integration has been the elimination of a number of first-rate black schools located in different parts of the country. These schools previously had produced a high proportion of eminent black Ph.D.s. The supporters of integration did not ask what conditions produce successful blacks, black scholars, professionals, and the like. They just assumed that all segregated schools were inferior to white or integrated schools.

HOROWITZ   Before attempting a specific response to the conservative argument that quality rather than quantity is what counts, it would be wise to place conservatism in a broader social context. Conservatism, from the antebellum South to the New Deal period, was largely a regional doctrine. One of its central assumptions has always been the right of regions and communities to a certain amount of self-determination and self-control. What has changed is the potency and power of the region. The South and Southwest, as they have increased in power, have amplified the conservative vantage point, given it a fiscal base.

Those industries that began as World War II industries, particularly the aircraft and atomic industries, were primarily located in the South, Southwest, and Far West—what has come to be known as the Southern Rim. These industries were always attached to American overseas activities and military participation abroad. Beyond that, Southern Rim industries rarely converted to peacetime productive activities. The Southern Rim, as a result, gave economic power and substance to the conservative ideology. It has remained a source of conservative strength for at least forty years.

At the same time, older industries that did, in fact, convert from peacetime to wartime efforts converted back when the war ended. Automobile manufacturers were capable of tank manufacturing; but when the war came to an end, automobiles were again the main source of economic strength. It was the responsiveness of the older industries located in the Northern Tier that produced what has been called the dominant liberal ideology. The fats and fortunes of the liberal ideology are tied to these older industries and banks. Too often we speak of ideology as if it was an unattached entity, failing to realize the economic bases of such ideological expressions. As a result of the transformation of the agrarian South to the industrial South and the drying up of older commodity production in the Northeast it is no longer correct to speak of American business ideology as essentially liberal. That is to say, the American business ideology has not so much dissolved as it has bifurcated along liberal and conservative axes. Not only do we have the rise of the Southern Rim and the stagnation of the Northern Tier, but also we have seen the emergence, the almost inexorable increase in size of a federal and state bureaucracy that has tended to underwrite a conservative viewpoint. The people who make their living in the bureaucratic network are directly linked to the kind of government-underwritten state capitalism more easily at home in Southern conservative thought than in Northern liberal thought. If I am correct, we can no longer speak of America as embodying a dominant liberal ideology; rather it is involved in a struggle between ideologies, with older and newer sectors of the business community lining up on liberal and conservative wings.

As for Tom Sowell's thesis on the decline of quality education within the black communities, this is merely an extension of the older conservative doctrine that mass education reduces and eventually eliminates standards of educational excellence. Such an argument would return education to a narrow band of elites and consign black people and other minorities to a toiler status. But such arbitrary distinctions between thinkers and toilers, head-workers and hand-workers, serves only to accentuate inequality in America. It is the problem and not the solution. Besides, whether in fact older educational techniques produced excellence or reinforced traditionalism remains to be determined. Certainly, such traditional models strongly tend to sacrifice innovation on the shoals of inheritance, science on the altar of theology. And that is quite a price to pay for the restoration of elite education.

QUESTION   Professor Horowitz, in your book, *Three Worlds of Development*, you raised the interesting issue of overdevelopment, or misdevelopment. One definition of it that you gave is "not paying close enough attention to social utility versus economic utility." I would like to ask both of you to what extent you think that conventional politics in the United States can deal with this problem of misdevelopment or overdevelopment, and, if politics cannot deal with it in the conventional way, how is it going to be dealt with?

HOROWITZ   In that volume I was concerned with the problem of overdevelopment as an economic phenomenon; namely, the underutilization of human resources and plant capacities. It is interesting that you should place the concept of overdevelopment in relation to the political superstructure, although, I daresay, this is a perfectly valid inference from my work. My feeling is that Weber is probably correct: when one examines the growth of social classes in the twentieth century, one finds that it is neither the proletarian nor the bourgeoisie that has maximal growth, but rather the bureaucratic sector that has uniquely expanded throughout our century. If we simply employ an operational definition of bureaucracy and mean those whose paychecks derive from the public sector, whether they are teachers and administrators at state colleges and universities or privates and generals in the armed forces, the size of the bureaucracy is immense. Nor is size the only problem. From an economic point of view, the bureaucracy is marginally productive, and that is one form of overdevelopment. From a political point of view, as I said before, it tends as a group to be conservative and reinforce the idea of the state as the most competent element in society, rather than the idea of social class.

The enormous increase in educated sectors of the population, the huge tenfold increase of the college educated and college bred in the last thirty years, also tends to propel large numbers into this bureaucratic sector. Thus, the growth of the bureaucratic class is largely unproductive economically; conservative politically; and it feeds on itself culturally. I would say that your question is correct: there is a sense in which overdevelopment and misdevelopment have penetrated American society at every level.

LIPSET   I would agree; but this increase in state power in large part fosters some of the basic problems of democracy and development that face us. There is another aspect to the question that I would like to mention briefly: the problem of growth. We have just hit the point where there are four billion people in the world. Some have become concerned in the last few years that America, or the world, is running out of resources. We are faced again with the old Malthusian argument that there are not enough natural resources to provide for a seemingly unlimited increase in population.

At this point, there are various demands from both outside and within the country that we limit growth either because of the problem of limited resources, or because its advocates believe that growth has had all sorts of dysfunctional consequences, particularly with respect to the environment, overcrowding, dirt, and the like. Governor Brown and many others have picked up the concept that "small is beautiful, small is better." But if it is true that we can no longer grow, that we have to live at whatever level we are at at the present moment, then one of the preconditions that everyone assumed is necessary for a better world is out the window. For Marx and others, abundance is a precondition for a truly egalitarian society; at least, much greater abundance than currently exists anywhere in the world today.

The United States as a country has been able to come through various crises without disaster because, in large part, it has had a steadily expanding gross national product, which meant ever-mounting prosperity. We have about eight to nine times the GNP per capita we had at the turn of the century. This has meant that the people at the bottom could always get more because there was a bigger pie to distribute. If the pie is no longer going to expand nationally or internationally, the only way the people can improve their situation is to take from one group and give to the other. That kind of politics will be much more crisis-ridden, a much more tense politics than ever before.

QUESTION   Professor Lipset, would you elaborate what fundamental changes this new intelligentsia you speak about brought about in society?

LIPSET   Joseph Schumpeter, the famous economist and sociologist, wrote intelligently about the phenomenon of the intellectual as a critic—the rise of the intelligentsia—in his book *Capitalism, Socialism and Democracy,* making the prediction that capitalism was doomed, that it would be destroyed inevitably and succeeded by some kind of socialist society. This, of course, was similar to the prediction that Marx made. But Schumpeter delivered it from a very different ideological perspective. Schumpeter, for one thing, did not look forward to socialism. He was a liberal economist in the classical sense. He believed that capitalism was a more efficient economic system than socialism, that socialism would be a step backwards. He thought capitalism worked well, that it was the most efficient possible system to raise productivity, and that a bureaucratic socialist state would result in a decrease in productivity.

Schumpeter argued that capitalism was doomed because he believed that no matter how efficient capitalism is, it can never win the allegiance of the intellectuals, who basically determine the ideas of the social system, provide legitimacy, and are able to define what is right and wrong about a culture. Intellectuals reject the materialistic criteria of success, of economic efficiency or of bourgeois solidity. They are bored by capitalism. Their interest in high culture leads them to be antimaterialistic and antibusiness. Consequently, he foresaw a constant nibbling away by the intelligentsia that would undermine the legitimacy of bourgeois or capitalist society.

Daniel Bell, in a recent book entitled *The Cultural Contradictions of Capitalism,* makes the same argument. Patrick Moynihan and Irving Kristol also have elaborated Schumpeter's analysis. Fundamentally, Schumpeter was right. I do not know whether he was correct that the intellectuals' attack will inevitably destroy capitalism per se and lead to its being replaced by socialism, but I agree that the values legitimating private enterprise are antithetical to the values of the bulk of the intellectual strata. The intellectual elite sees itself in opposition to the production elite. This is not only true in the Western world; it is true in the communist world as well.

Soviet intellectuals, of course, have much less freedom to express their hostility. Undermining the legitimacy of the production elite does make for change. Ironically, the biggest change it fosters is the aspect Professor Horowitz is most worried about—the growth of the bureaucratic state. Fundamentally, in Western society the intelligentsia view the state more positively than they do business, since the state is a nonprofit, noncommercial institution. They see it as the expression of the community operating for welfare objectives, and they therefore basically support its growth. Consequently, the increased influence of the intelligentsia, reflected in the growing importance of the university world and the media world, helps to de-legitimate the traditional rationale of the old-fashioned production sector of society in our society of business and capitalism.

QUESTION   You gentlemen described the composition of American society, in the first part of your discussion of American political parties, and in the second part you described the composition of American life in terms of competing values: of liberty on the one hand, and of equality on the other. I believe it is appropriate for a sociologist to describe the composition of things. Then I would go beyond it and ask you: What is it that you would have a political leader do? Or is it such that because of the composition of our parties as you would see it—five parts, three parts—or the composition of our life in terms of competing values, is it impossible for a leader to do anything?

HOROWITZ   While it is fair to say that it is one thing for a social scientist to describe, and another for the political leader to prescribe, the problem at the moment is to identify the leadership. The impulse for bureaucracy is so extensive and the power of middle management in government so great that I do not believe we can any longer speak of an imperial presidency moving us in any one direction. Quite beyond the changing relationship between bureaucracy and leadership is the fact that we may not be living in great times. We like to assume that the present moment has a unique excitement to it. But these great events are, for the most part, manufactured events with only a twenty-four hour durability. Elsewhere I have written about the twentieth century as having much more in common with what Barbara Tuchman describes as characteristics of the fourteenth century: war, plague, pestilence, and the like, rather than a thirteenth-century City of God.

As a result, it becomes dangerous even to formulate questions in terms of advice for leadership. If, in fact, there is a long-standing malaise, those whom we define as leaders can either point to the malaise and perform a cleansing ritual or they can become part of the problem itself. I always find it strange that when we demand action, the man of knowledge is seen as stepping out of his role. I do not believe it is realistic to say what leadership can do since what we are suffering through is not a failure of leadership so much as a failure of systems. This is not simply an American problem; the erosion of faith in socialism has come about with the realization of the systemic weaknesses of Soviet society. The erosion of faith in capitalism has come about similarly with an indication of weaknesses in American society. Before we can speak of what leadership can do, we must stipulate the systemic limits within which leaders and followers alike are bound to each other for better or worse.

II. EQUALITY

HOROWITZ   The problem of equality, the state of being equal, is linked to the problem of equity, the quality of being fair and just. For while the two are organically related, indeed, often spoken of as isomorphic, being fair and simultaneously making sure that everyone in a society has the same life chances is no easy matter. Add to that a built-in ambiguity between equality in starting positions (i.e., everyone should have the same opportunity) and equality of outcomes (everyone should be guaranteed a decent standard of living and security), and one begins to see that what appears at first to be a self-evident proposition is in fact a complex, often cross-purpose abstraction.

For the purposes of our dialogue, it may be wisest and simplest to avoid nitpicking at the conceptual level and get on with the task of studying equality in America, taking for granted that the question of how society can best achieve equity is a global concern. As a concept, equality has an infinite number of meanings. For example, even were we to accomplish full job satisfaction and participation among our black citizens, or full equality in economic terms for women in the labor force, we would still be faced with the problems of other minorities: problems of the aged, the young, and a variety of other subgroups. Were we to resolve the employment problem for those groups discriminated against because of sex, age, race, and nationality, we would then, surely, move on to other problems, for example, the rights of fat people and skinny people; short people and tall people; the rights of animals; the rights of subjects of research. With respect to equity, one can argue the case for whatever cause one happens to believe in. In this way, civil rights issues impede civil liberties—a dangerous treadmill.

If equity were every fully realized, it would mean that, in effect, we would all start in the race of life at the same place and the fastest would win. The problem with the imagery of a footrace is that it leaves unclear whether the better and swifter should win, or whether the hurdles should be set so that we all end together. There is a starting point concept of equity and a terminal point concept of equity. But if we get beyond the epistemological hurdle we still have the problem of the rise of contrary demands. At this point, environmental groups, ecological groups, population control groups, and abortion groups all favor zero growth or limited growth. For these groups, high, rapid-paced growth is highly stressful;* to ease the sense of stress we must limit the amount, the pace, and even the quality of growth, as they see it.

Often the same people who champion the rights of women or blacks also defend environmental protection agency controls and population control mechanisms; in other words, they advocate limited growth. But those who want to limit growth do not necessarily want to redistribute the present economic pie. With an infinite economic growth—or at least a rapidly expanding pie—the problem

---

*See Jay W. Forrester *World Dynamics*. (Cambridge, Mass: Wright Allen Publishers, 1971); and "Limits to Growth Revisited," *Journal of the Franklin Institute*. Whole no. 30, no. 2 (August 1975), pp. 107–111.

of taking a portion from one person and giving it to another does not arise. When, however, the size of that pie is limited, then the problem becomes one of distribution. Then one finds a sharp antagonism between those who maintain that the quality of life has deteriorated because of the continuing growth of the economic pie and those who maintain that there remain unsatisfied demands that are constitutionally guaranteed.

At present we are confronted with a policy problem of enormous magnitude. This problem is made even more complex by the kinds of theorizing we have dealt with, which are primarily neo-Marxian and neo-Keynesian paradigms. Both assume affluence, if not opulence, and both assume a continued expansion of technological growth, energy resources, and energy availabilities. Both categorically deny the neo-Malthusian framework of pestilence, war, and shortages of resources.

In the world of sociology, little attention is given to questions of scarcity. There are assumptions of abundance; consequently when we have an oil boycott or a shortage of basic minerals, the shock is enormous and the fallout, in policy and in social research terms, is considerable. This leads us to the question of whether we can even make accurate predictions about the year 1980, never mind the year 2000. When we entered this decade, the literature hardly mentioned the possibility of limited resources, or the idea of limits. Only now is the concept of affluence being challenged as a geographical or ecological reality.

If we pose the problem accurately we can, at least, work our way out of the woods. The problem is that we have two powerful, contrasting paradigms: one, an infinite demand for equity; the second, an equally powerful demand for finite, if not zero growth.

LIPSET If you look at the problem of equality in the American context—for that matter, in the world context—the term has had a number of meanings. The two most essential are equality of opportunity and equality of condition. The former is the equal right of individuals to get ahead, to determine whatever position they can attain in career terms. Equality of condition, or what has become to be known in recent years as equality of result, is a modern version of the old communist notion: from each according to his ability, to each according to his needs. That is, people get what they need. Society does not differentiate in reward.

In American society, and in the socialist and communist countries as well, the emphasis in practice, though not in ideals, has been on equality of opportunity. That has been what Americans have meant when they talked about this being an egalitarian society. Some suggest a third meaning—equality of respect, which is independent of the other two. This is what Tocqueville and other foreign travelers described when they said that Americans, regardless of the tremendous actual difference in status or income, treated each other as individuals who deserved respect. They were amazed that servants and members of the lower strata did not have to bow down or show deference.

One of the strongest indications of how powerful equality of opportunity has been as a political ideology is its appearance as the credo of the first Workingmen's party, so named, in the world. The Workingmen's party was formed in New York, Philadelphia, and a number of other eastern cities in the late 1820s. The New York party, which was the strongest, actually proposed in what would be, even by our contemporary standards, a very sophisticated document that all children be sent to state-supported boarding schools away from home. The party literature noted that the opportunity for all children, rich and poor, to go to the same school (what we now term an integrated school), was not enough to guarantee equality of opportunity. Children coming from rich, well-to-do, better-educated families had a stimulating environment—were culturally superior, to use modern phraseology—while others were deprived.

They then actually proposed that all children be put in the same environment for twenty-four hours a day to guarantee equality of opportunity. This meant taking the children away from their parents and sending them to state-supported boarding schools. They proposed that children from the age of six attend such schools. I submit that this proposal was the most radical ever made by a political party, one that makes the programs of contemporary socialist-communist parties seem moderate.

What they were proposing was a program not to nationalize property, but to nationalize children. And the Workingmen's party actually received something like 15 percent of the vote in New York. They elected some members to the legislature and the city council. While this was clearly a utopian proposal which has been forgotten, it indicates the strength, at that early period in the nation's history, with which some people believed in the necessity of equalizing opportunity for the underprivileged. This idea was, of course, expressed at the same time that America was still a slave society. But the effort to make the emphasis on equality of opportunity a reality was powerful and it has remained strong throughout American history.

What has historically enabled Americans to move up is not the particular value system of the society but the fact of an expanding population, an expanding economic structure, and, in particular, mass immigration. Studies that have been made of the occupational position of immigrants, using U.S. Census data, indicate that the immigrants generally came to America from Europe (though some came from Asia) with little education and little skill so that they appeared here first at the bottom of the social structure. They brought muscle power and they took unskilled labor jobs.

By taking these jobs at the bottom they made it possible for native-born Americans—the children of the previous generation of immigrants—to move up. Many of the immigrants felt reasonably happy because in a sense they moved up also, not socially but to a higher standard of living than they had known in Europe or Japan. Their children did much better, and their grandchildren, the third generation, tended to do as well or better than old stock Americans.

Mass immigration lasted into the 1920s. It virtually stopped completely in the depression, which caused all kinds of problems, but since World War II there has been a migration pattern within North America that encourages mobility. Blacks, Puerto Ricans, and, to some extent, southern whites—the American peasantry—have moved into the cities. Millions of Mexicans and other Latin Americans have also entered the U.S. Finally, it should be noted that women as a group have played a role similar to that of immigrants or blacks in the occupational system. They have taken the less-privileged jobs; they constitute the white-collar proletariat. Telephone operators, secretaries, key-punch operators, nurses, teachers in the elementary schools— these are lower level jobs held by women. In taking these jobs they have permitted men, often their fathers, husbands, and sons, to have better positions.

The upshot of these processes in statistical terms, as reported in very good studies of social mobility in recent decades by Dudley Duncan, Robert Hauser, and Christopher Jencks, is the initially surprising finding that the United States comes very close to equality of opportunity for white males. Family background makes some difference for this group but not very much. Christopher Jencks and a group of his colleagues who analyzed income data found that the difference between brothers and totally unrelated randomly selected men was of the order of only $500 a year. That is, the income difference between that received by any two unrelated men and that reported for the average pair of brothers was $500. This points up how little difference family background seems to make for white males, but it must be stressed the picture is quite different for blacks, Chicanos, and women. The latter groups contribute heavily to the lower rungs of the structure.

Those now entering at the bottom, however, are faced with the possibility that there may not be any new recruits after them. The blacks and the white peasants may have no replacements on the bottom. The demand for equal rights by women and blacks, if successful, means that white males will hold fewer high-level jobs in a stable population with limited migration from foreign and non-urban areas. It is possible, of course, that the technological or occupational structure will continue to be upgraded, that the number of low-level occupations will continue to decline, while the number of jobs requiring high levels of education and technological training will increase. These processes imply a class structure that looks like a diamond rather than a pyramid. With technological development, society shifts from a pyramid, where most positions are at the bottom, to a diamond, where most positions are in the middle. Such changes as mass immigration mean more upward than downward movement from one generation to another.

These kinds of structural changes, which have gone on for many generations, seem to have slowed down considerably. As I noted earlier, this means that any further progress toward equality will require an increase in downward mobility. If some move up, others have to move down. If women move up, men have to move down proportionately. If you have a situation where the women's role in the occupational structure has been on the average much lower than the men's—if the women then move up so that they exist in the same proportions in occupations as the general population or labor force, then a certain proportion of men have to have lower jobs than in the previous generation. If blacks and Chicanos move up in a nonexpanding society with no new immigrants or migrants coming in, then a certain number of whites have to come down.

These developments are beginning to occur, and they are beginning to hurt. There are complaints and concerns about them, particularly in relation to government affirmative action programs designed to implement equality of result with respect to sex and race. Equality, in other words, is beginning to cost. It is not just a free good, as in a certain sense it was a kind of psychic as well as technical free good in the expanding population of the past. As a result, we may begin to have a considerable degree of tension in the next generation, or even in the present one. This is obviously a very real problem to those who are students; they will graduate soon and will have to go out into the labor market. They are undoubtedly aware of the changed situation from ten or fifteen years ago. One reason for the change is the fact that there are more women in the labor force. It is necessary to recognize this.

The number of employed people in the United States today is at an all-time high. The labor force is larger than ever before because of the tremendous increase in the 1960s of young people; but even more, it has grown because of the great increase in the number of women who are ready to take jobs, who are trained for jobs. Insofar as there has been an increase in the number of such women, considerably above the normal growth of the labor force, to have full employment would require a much larger increase in the number of jobs than has ever developed previously.

It is unfortunately true that one of the major causes of recession, particularly for the better educated, is the incursion of women into the labor force. We are now in a situation in which some people (women) get more, while others (men) must receive less. In the context of a limited-growth economy, women's liberation is painful for a lot of men, particularly white males. In fact, black females are doing much better than black males, and the better educated among them—those just out of college—are doing better than white males. We welcome progress, but we sometimes forget the strains that accompany it. Improvement in the black situation adversely affects some whites.

Take the fact that as of 1976 the percentage of blacks entering college as freshmen was actually higher than the percentage of blacks in the general population. The Census reports that 12.6 percent of the entering freshmen in 1975 were blacks, an incredible statistic given the past history of educational deprivation for the black population. It is true that one has to add very quickly most of those black freshmen are not going to the same kinds of schools as the average white student. They are disproportionately concentrated in black colleges in the South, and in community and junior colleges—schools not as good academically as those most whites attend.

But, still, it is a tremendous advance to be able to discuss a situation where blacks are going to college in roughly the same proportion as they are in the population as a whole. The percentage of blacks graduating is still considerably less than that of whites. But the absolute gain in numbers means that blacks are competing for jobs that once were the sole domain of whites. And in a nonexpanding labor market, if blacks increase their share of the good jobs, then some whites will get less. They are going to resent it, they will feel frustrated and embittered. As we move toward equality of opportunity in the real sense for everyone—black and white, men and women—we must learn that equality of success also means equality of failure. In an open society, one has to remember that the number of good jobs, the number of prestigious, highly rewarded positions, is a minority of the total number of positions. If every college graduate wants to have a pretty good job (and there just are not that many high-level jobs around); if women college graduates refuse to become housewives, and they compete for jobs that were formerly male preserves, then we will witness increased frustration among their male counterparts.

HOROWITZ   You have described a revolution of falling expectations. Many of us have grown up in a world of Stevensonian rhetoric that embodies a revolution of rising expectations and depends on the infinite expansion of the GNP. Meeting these expectations comes upon the fact of finite energy resources.

Can a society and can a population participate in a revolution of falling expectations? What does it imply? Does it mean having a car longer, rather than trading it in every year, or owning your home at forty rather than when you are first married? Perhaps the house itself will be smaller, with fewer amenities. Can U.S. society as a whole move in the direction of diminished expectations, or is this a selective process in which some people participate and others do not? That is to say, one unanswered question is, how many people are actually willing to participate in a revolution of declining expectations?

Some people have the money to pay for what have become luxuries. There are, after all, those for whom fifty-five cents for a gallon of gas is marginal to their household economy or to their sense of security. There are others for whom a dollar per gallon of gas would mean a great sacrifice. There are some who can still afford large luxury cars, and clearly there is still such a market. In every area there are those who can, in fact, afford the luxuries of life. Despite the contradiction between demands for equity and for zero growth, a stratum of the population has become even more visibly affluent.

One of the marvels of American life historically has been the kind of invisible affluence wealthy Americans have been able to generate. Yet, in an odd way, wealthy Americans have really violated the Veblen thesis by disguising their wealth. If you scrutinize young people in any college or university, you will have a hard time determining who has personal family wealth and who does not, something that any European could immediately determine on the basis of clothing and mannerisms. The rise of a methodology for measuring unobtrusive measures is a response to a democracy of style. Now, all of a sudden, decreased economic growth creates a visible economic elite that has the potential to become an object of aggression. Class rivalry and class warfare is a much more earnest and bitter possibility in a world of scarce resources than in one marked by unlimited natural wealth.

LIPSET There is an interesting point about the affluent advocating no growth. Much of the advocacy of no growth—a cleaner environment, ecological decency—comes from well-educated, well-to-do people who are concerned about protecting certain environments from overcrowding, dirt, and similar problems. But in many cases the environments they are protecting are ones to which they, and not the underprivileged, have access. By limiting further development, they are depriving not themselves but the less privileged.

For example, Cape Cod was declared a National Seashore under a bill passed under Kennedy declaring that the existing density of housing could not increase. This law also resulted in existing houses on Cape Cod consequently going up three or four times in value because these had become a much scarcer commodity. Cape Cod is a wonderful place; but should access to it be limited to a relatively small number of affluent individuals? Those who summer on Martha's Vineyard are now involved in a comparable effort. If you visit Martha's Vineyard, you will find that people there are outraged that the Martha's Vineyard Boat Company advertises for day-trip visitors. Those who own summer homes there do not want more people. But only a few thousand people own homes on Martha's Vineyard, and if the legislation that has been introduced by Senator Kennedy as an extension of the Cape Cod bill passes, they will have a monopoly on this nice environment.

There are many two-, three-, or four-acre summer plots. If these are subdivided into plots of one-half acre, one-quarter acre, or smaller, the result will be increased density of population, destruction of nature, and more pollution—but a lot more people will have access to a better life in the summer. The issue is whether to keep these and other comparable areas clean and nice for a relatively few rich people or to increase the density and dirt, and thereby give many more people the opportunity to live more decent lives. It is ironic that many people who consider themselves liberal or left politically are defending their right to special privileges, to holding the masses down as part of what they believe is a liberal program.

The labor movement has tended in recent years to be very much opposed to many of the ecological demands of the conservationists because the trade unions put jobs ahead of cleanliness. They are ready to take a considerable amount of pollution, if cutting down on pollution means reducing the number of jobs. Well-to-do people who do not have to worry about jobs quite properly worry about pollution; but to those for whom a job is a necessary condition for supporting their families, pollution may be a price worth paying. Affluent people, many of whom think of themselves as supporters of the left, simply do not understand that for others the alternative to pollution is unemployment and worse, if it involves shutting down factories or eliminating access routes to work places.

These questions are real political issues, not hypothetical ones. In California, in June 1976, the voters overwhelmingly defeated an initiative proposal put on the ballot by liberal conservationist forces to severely hamstring the operation of nuclear energy plants. The organized labor movement was the chief force opposing the proposal. They want nuclear energy, not because they like nuclear energy per se or because they have, for some reason, a different view of the dangers involved, but because they recognize that nuclear energy means cheaper and more abundant power; cheaper power means more factories; more factories mean more jobs. Evaluating the risks and other trade-offs, the voters chose jobs over cleanliness. The conflict is a real class issue, even though many of the more well-to-do people pressing for conservation, ecology, no growth, a cleaner environment, etc., see themselves fighting for a better, cleaner American society—not recognizing that, for the less privileged, cleanliness is not the supreme virtue.

HOROWITZ   Ecology is also in part a racial issue. In East St. Louis there is (or was) a large chemical plant that was burning soft (bituminous) coal, which is relatively inexpensive but burns incompletely, or dirtier, for the most part. The plant was asked by the local EPA to use hard (anthracite) coal, which burns more cleanly to turn out its products. The wind currents created by the more rapidly burning hard coal brought the chemical reagent, or the chemical agents, from East St. Louis to St. Louis. St. Louis's EPA argued for a changeover to anthracite.

The consequence was that the corporation delivered an ultimatum that they would have to leave if they were forced to burn anthracite rather than bituminous because of the cost of the changeover. In point of fact, they did leave; one of the plants shut down. East St. Louis is a small urban community with extraordinarily high unemployment. Ninety-five percent of the people who worked in the plant were black, and the closing of this plant put another 500 or 600 black proletarians on the labor market. So the clash between the Environmental Protection Agency and the trade union movement in practice issues into a heavy racial as well as class antagonism, which certainly cannot be dismissed. Again, it is not a question of right and wrong, but of competing demands.

I would add that there are new concepts of what equality and equity are about, removing these concepts from the sphere of social mobility and moving them into what you might call socialist scripture. Now the problem of equity demands is linked very often to demands of ethnic minority groups, of women as a sexual group, of all kinds of phenomena having to do with birthright claims: religiosity, race, and sex. The breakdown, the limits of continued upward mobility, have led to a resurrection of ascribed values that, in their own way, inhibit social reform.

They do so, first, because ascribed values make a claim on society, not in the name of the normal channels of achievement orientations or movement toward equality but in the name of maximizing advantages within a racial group or within an ethnic minority. And that produces yet a more complex, even more anguishing problem. What is to be the central thrust of American demands for equity? If our society is to becme pluralist, then it is pluralism and fragmentation along racial or sexual lines. What, then, is the inner core of equity values within American life? Do they exist? And can they be retained? We are dealing with an entire panoply of problems as we enter the third century where a definite set of contradictory demands has led, in my opinion, to a breakup of the paradigms with which we have come to live. Resolving these competing demands is where a considerable amount of energy is going to have to be invested.

We must define more precisely what we mean by equity; we must envision an achievement orientation—the son outdoing the father, the daughter outdoing the mother—in terms of mobility in the economic ladder and in contrast to a notion of ethnic homogeneity, or religious homogeneity that espouses the larger national culture. In the contradiction between equality and equity demands it becomes incumbent upon us to take more seriously the possibility of breakup of our national culture through disintegration rather than breakup through revolution.

The problem at the top is the increasing visibility of those who are affluent; the problem at the bottom is the growing difficulty of isolating and examining the underclass. Beyond that point we have new forms of struggle at the bottom that were much more muted in the nineteenth century than in the twentieth century. We used to talk in terms of a lumpenproletariat, in terms of residual capacity or residual phenomena within the society. Now we've changed all of that for a respectable designation: marginals, or marginal groupings. We now have a struggle between what you might call an underclass and a working class—that is, between those whose revenues are largely derived from marginal occupational activities that have mushroomed in an urban context and from all kinds of state benefits and programs, and those who continue in the labor force as proletarians. Now we really do not have at this point a rhetoric to explain the breakdown of equity at this level, and the emergence of interest groups who see other interest elements as rivals for a shrinking pie.

How does one address a member of the working class who comes home with $150, and how does one convince that person that the individual who receives welfare benefits or food stamps, which net out to $115, should not, in some sense, be considered an enemy, to be blunt about it? How does one create forms of cohesion between those competing groups at the bottom of the ladder? We have a series of complicated but at the same time fundamental issues that could very easily tear American society apart. Questions that we are posing about equality are not reducible to the bigger the better, or the more the merrier, or to making do with less, or small is beautiful. They point to the incompatibility of many simultaneously expressed demands, or at any rate, the failure on the part of social science to resolve what appears to be this incompatibility.

LIPSET   If I may pick up a related topic on these problems of the future—for me, one of the saddest statements known to man, one that nobody I know of understands how to challenge or change, no matter what alternative social system or reform or revolution they would like to see—is that 50 percent of any population is always below the median. Now that trite observation, which is important in the context of thinking of an open egalitarian society, is a very unhappy statement, because it means that 50 percent are going to be in the lower half, indeed, *must* be in the less-privileged half as long as society is stratified in any way in terms of reward, status, good positions, more interesting jobs, and kinds of education received.

For most of human history, i.e., in ancient slave societies, in the feudal system, the Indian caste system, and others, populations have been stratified. In such societies, even those in which there was some mobility, most people were brought up to believe that they were in an appropriate position by virtue of their birth—that their birthright status was all they could have, and that they should try to do well in whatever station they were born to. But modern industrial society has rejected ascription and fostered a belief in achievement. We now have open achievement-oriented social systems—those of North America, western Europe, and the Communist world—in which many more than half the population want to be in the upper half.

Many more than a quarter of the population want to be in the upper quarter. Children socialized in these societies are taught that they can reach high level positions, can succeed, if they study and work hard.

How do societies deal with the gap between desired and attainable statuses? In some countries, the Soviet Union for example, this has become a real problem, calling for government policy. The Soviets have allowed high school education to expand with demand. As many Soviet youth as want to can attend and graduate from high schools. But the number of openings in universities, in higher education, has not expanded with demand. At the present time, something like five or six times as many Soviet high school graduates seek to gain entrance to colleges and universities as there are places. This means five out of six just cannot go. They take the entrance exams, but only one of six qualifies for higher education. The Soviets have a stratified educational system, much like ours, with better and worse colleges, specialized schools, and prestigious ones that are very selective in admissions. But no matter how well Soviet youth do in high school, most cannot go on to college because the state limits entrance places to the number of college or university graduates needed by the economy. This problem does not occur in planned communist societies only. In Western Germany a similar situation exists today. Many more Germans graduate from high school than are admitted into universities.

What happens to those who want to go to universities but cannot? There is little doubt that they are terribly unhappy people. Soviet writers, sociologists, and others have described the problem. Many of the ambitious rejectees will not go to work. The Soviets face a real problem with high school graduates who refuse to take regular jobs.

They know that almost all the good jobs in society go to college graduates. As a result, unless and until they can get into college, many wander around refusing to be absorbed into the regular labor force.

The Japanese have a similar phenomenon among their youth. They call them *Ronin,* the masterless people, after the masterless Samurai of medieval Japan. The United States and a number of Western countries postpone this problem since they treat college and university the way the Soviets do high school, that is, allowing higher education to expand to the limit of demand. People may not be admitted into the colleges they desire, but almost everybody who wants to gets into some institution. The problem faced by these societies is an increasing number of people with college degrees who constitute an ever greater number of applicants for the kinds of jobs associated with college degrees than exist. The situation has been exacerbated by the increase in the number of women college graduates who want to go to work.

In future years, a larger and larger proportion of the college graduate population will have to accept jobs at much lower skill, income, and status levels. This means, of course, that there will be increasing numbers of people frustrated individually. I use the word individually rather than collectively because I think they will see themselves as failures rather than feel that there is something wrong with the society because it has not provided a niche for them. In a sense, the more egalitarian a stratified society is in terms of equality of opportunity, the more frustrated people it will contain. The only egalitarian society that would not sustain such frustrations is the sort of social system that ideal communism supposedly would be—one where there are no stratified rewards.

But clearly, regardless of what one may think possible in some ultimate future, communism in this sense is not going to exist in any human society within the lifetime of any of us here, and probably well beyond that. The Marxian conditions for communism—abundance and the elimination of manual work by machines—are a long way off. The increase in opportunity, the growth in equality of opportunity, will therefore increase frustration. More equality means more failures; more failures, more frustration.

This syllogism brings up the problems faced by those categories of people who previously were allocated the lower jobs of the society by ascription but who now respond to the promise of equal opportunity. When very few blacks could look forward to the opportunity to go to college or get decent jobs, those blacks who had steady jobs as laborers, postmen, or Pullman porters were doing well within the context of their own racial group. A black did not have to feel like a failure for being a Pullman porter or a postman, since he knew, and those around him knew, that the occupational horizons of blacks were largely limited to such positions. When few girls were able to get into medical school, those who became nurses were doing pretty well. They were part of the high-status medical complex. Now that more women are going to medical school to become physicians, it is easy to anticipate that nurses are going to be more frustrated and less satisfied with their jobs. The only way to ease this situation is to increase the number of men in the nursing profession, so that the identification of nursing as a lower-status woman's profession changes.

These kinds of problems in societies moving toward increased equality of opportunity are rarely anticipated. Some psychiatrists, for example, suggest that recent increases of certain kinds of mental illness among blacks are strongly related to a sense of personal failure that blacks in lower-status jobs are now experiencing. The same tendency has been noticed among women. Many have written about those who have remained housewives and mothers and the problems posed by the demotion of these roles as a consequence of the movement toward sexual equality. There are many women who are "only housewives and mothers," and they tend increasingly to be looked down upon by working women, particularly by professional women with careers. They have become failures.

Similarly, as more women attain prestigious occupational roles once held solely by men, many women in traditional women's occupations, like secretaries and telephone operators, will feel inferior and unhappy about their roles in life. Twenty and thirty years ago, these women would not have felt this way. It is going to take a long time for these kinds of relationships affecting status satisfaction to sort themselves out. It is unfortunate yet necessary to recognize that even if we believe that in the long run more equality of opportunity makes for a more happy society, it is not necessarily true that it has the same effect in the short run.

HOROWITZ   Sometimes the problem of stratification is met by a process of relabeling, as a prelude to reorienting actual incomes. Persons once called garbagemen are now given the title "sanitation engineers." A person who used to be called a truck driver can now be called a truck chauffeur. This is not just verbal sleight of hand, for as labels are changed economic rewards are altered. When sanitation engineers make almost as much,, if not as much as professors, then the status incongruity between the sanitation engineer and the professor diminishes; and so too do inherited distinctions between head work and hand work.

One can easily see how someone with an advanced degree could go into sanitation engineering. Some occupations, like hotel management, until a few years ago were really residual activities that people went into by virtue of the fact that there was not much else available. Now we have sophisticated schools of hotel management. In some sense, the solution to the problem of equality involves a changing notion regarding what is considered to be a desirable occupation. Label changes will stick if they are tied to economic advancement, especially for those people who up to now have been disadvantaged. Similarly, if the wages and salaries of college professors are held relatively constant, and, at the same time, large-scale wage increases and fringe benefits are made available to the Teamsters, for instance, there is no doubt that within a few years equal salary possibilities for truck drivers and academics would result. There will still be marginal benefits in being a professor, like long summers. On the other hand, that benefit is counterbalanced by the security in trade union work vis-à-vis the insecurity of an untenured position. The real problem thus shifts from status incongruity to the difficulty in motivating people to engage in creative work while denying them the traditional fiscal advantages of such endeavors.

We have to begin to address these kinds of issues more frankly and not simply throw up our hands and recite a lexicon of contradictions within American society. As Professor Lipset said earlier, equality hurts those who have, and hurting those who have becomes the name of the political game. This is going to be an interesting period because those who have been nominally identified with liberal and radical causes will be the ones most often hurt by financial rearrangements. And the ones who will be assisted often will be those who have not been so identified. So it will be intriguing indeed to see how ideology or ideological prerequisites are squared with a growing impulse toward equity on a much broader scale than we have hitherto experienced.

LIPSET   There is an interesting development (I have no sense of how widespread it is in statistical terms, though it is quite visible in university communities such as the Boston-Cambridge area, Berkeley, Madison, Ann Arbor, and others) involving persons marginal to the university or intellectual worlds who try to maintain an identity as graduate students, who seek to remain associated with the intellectual community. In order to maintain this fringe role, they work at various jobs that are non-intellectual.

I am told, for example, that the auto industry in Detroit, which has a lot of trouble getting people to work on Mondays, Fridays, and weekends, employs a large number of part-time "students" who are ready to work a couple of days a week. For many of these people, the real part of their life is their identity as a student, their involvement in books, intellectual discussions, and living in communes. Since they have to earn some money, they take jobs, but the jobs for them are secondary, not their real identity. It does not matter to them, therefore, what they do to earn money—whether they are waiters, janitors, or on the assembly line—that is all secondary.

Such behavior is an example of withdrawal from the competitive structure of an economy in which many try but few succeed. It is a rejection of the competitive ethos, an escape into the fringe economy. On the other hand, some ideological veterans of the anticompetitive movement of the sixties are now to be found in small businesses. These are run, ironically, by people who still think of themselves as being anticapitalist. They start restaurants, farms, or artisan shops. Many of them see themselves rejecting capitalism, escaping from the materialist economy, because by running a business they are not working for someone else. If they have to take jobs, they prefer ones like cab driver or postman, where they are not closely supervised.

It would be interesting and important to get a reliable estimate of how frequently this behavior occurs. My sense is that it is an increasingly popular phenomenon reflective of the new status conferred on those who voluntarily choose to opt out from full participation—full ego participation—in the competitive society. The rejectees say: "I am going to do my own thing," "I am going to express myself" in all sorts of ways that are not job related. Hence, my job will be only something I do to earn as much money as I need to maintain myself and no more. I do not want a steady job; I do not want a regular job. Obviously, this kind of behavior can be found only among young people. Presumably, as one gets older, it becomes increasingly difficult to maintain this fringe role. One wonders what has become of those people who have been doing these things for the last ten years.

A different kind of change, also resulting in part from the increased emphasis on equal opportunity for all, is the two-job family—a consequence of increased participation by women in the labor force. Among the college-educated young professionals, large numbers are married to others in roughly the same occupational category, which means that they are often earning, as a family unit, as much or more than an older professional whose wife does not work. This development affects the income distribution of the country, which is analyzed in terms of family income.

Ironically, the increased participation by women in the labor force serves to make the income distribution, as it is measured by the Census, less equal than it would be otherwise. When there are two or more breadwinners in a family, that family tends to be classified as relatively high in the income structure. This press toward greater income inequality has been intensified since the increase in the number of women working has occurred much more in the middle and upper classes, in the college graduate part of the population, than it has in the working class. Working-class women are not so attracted to the kinds of jobs they have that they want to continue working after they are married. Many women who are waitresses, key-punch operators, or workers on an assembly line look forward to escaping the boredom of their work by staying home with the children. Being a typist is no great deal. Women in low-status employment lack a sense of a career; similarly, they do not see holding down a monotonous job as a contribution to women's equality.

Those who are editors, executives, professors, teachers, or doctors form the basis of another story. Female professors, lawyers, doctors, and professional women generally want to work even after marriage. Hence, the amount of money in the hands of upper-middle-class families has increased. And, to repeat this ironic fact, increased participation by middle class women in the labor force has created a greater inequality of income distribution in the United States than in the 1950s when proportionally fewer women worked.

HOROWITZ   When we talk about marginal groups, we must not only talk about people who drive taxi cabs or work part-time in factories. We are overlooking, in some measure, the possibility of marginality in areas like prostitution, pimping, gambling, drug sales, and drug pushing. These have become big business phenomena in this culture and in this country, and they take up an enormous amount of marginal slack. When one talks about the culture of university life, or possible spin-offs, he is talking also about a phenomenon that is known in the Third World, but that we have not known here, which is the rise of urban marginality, or modernization without industrialization. Or, let us say modernization outpaces industrialization creating all kinds of marginal pigeonholes for all kinds of different people.

Now what does that do to a concept of equity or to the concept of work as the source of equity? I am reminded of what the economist Albert O. Hirschman has always said—there are two ways of looking at a product: one, by what goes into it, and the other, by what is the final result. It is easy to look at the final outcome, at a television or an automobile, and say, "I want it, I deserve it, I ought to have it." It is quite another to say, I have to work 454 man-hours to have the product. Now, if the choice is between working 454 man hours or pimping for 5 hours to get the same product, then there is going to be heavy pressure, it seems to me, on the marginal sector of the intelligentsia to move into that area. We are so heavily focused in our society on the problem of equity that perhaps we have lost sight of the problem of work. And the problem of the guarantee of equity through labor input and labor power may in fact be a source of the tension I was mentioning earlier between the marginals and the working classes. I cannot help but think that we have witnessed class antagonism at much sharper levels than we were led to expect by the liberal and Keynesian literature.

LIPSET   A lot of this is true. This relates to another problem that we have not talked about—crime. Higher crime rates are characteristic of societies that stress opportunity, which means, as I have emphasized, many failures as well as successes. The United States has had the highest crime rate of any country in the developed world. It is necessary to limit comparisons within this category since, obviously, problems of crime, wealth, and position in countries like India or Saudi Arabia are of a different magnitude. The rates of crime, of course, have steadily increased throughout the developed world, other countries as well as the United States. Britain, for example, which used to be a relatively crime-free country, has experienced considerable increases in its crime rates since World War II, although in total number of crimes committed, she is still behind us.

Social scientists like Robert Merton, have attempted to explain increased crime in modern, more affluent societies. These scholars have suggested that to some degree crime is a way of achieving economic goods without following the legitimate methods of study and work—institutionalized means that for many would not lead to a decent social position or income. Crime, as Dan Bell has stressed, is a mechanism of social mobility. Increased crime, therefore, may reflect a greater emphasis on equality. The more emphasis on equality of opportunity in a society, this analysis suggests, the higher the crime rate. Perhaps, therefore, the proverbial high crime rate in the United States is a tribute to the fact that we stressed equality of opportunity for all (white males) earlier than other countries. As a result, more Americans have felt frustrated as failures and have taken this illegitimate way to success.

The same processes appear to be at work in the Soviet Union. Although the Soviets do not issue crime statistics, it would appear that they too have been experiencing a steady, massive increase in rates of crime. In terms of Marxist theory, this should not occur, and the Soviets clearly do not understand why it is happening. But the assumption that greater stress on equality of opportunity increases frustration among the failures begins to supply reasons for increased crime in the USSR.

In most societies that claim to be open to talent, the kinds of jobs offered to young people, particularly those who do not have a decent education, are generally uninteresting and unrewarding positions, and young people do not want them. Some years ago, a sociologist, Ted Harwood, sought to analyze the sources of the large-scale unemployment among black teenagers in Houston. Harwood concluded that if you look at American teenagers, regardless of race, they do not like to work, and they do not want to work. In any case, the kinds of jobs available to them do not interest them much.

He argued that the way white young people, particularly middle-class ones, escape work is to go to school. That is the appropriate cultural response for them. At that time, he suggested, many young blacks came out of cultural backgrounds that did not find school to be a positive experience (it has often been a punitive experience for many of them). They drop out, but, like whites, they do not go to work. He suggests that, generally, those who are not socialized to the culture of the school in America drop out of school but refuse to go to work. Statistically, they are counted as teenage unemployed. But many of them could have jobs, low-level ones to be sure, but regular employment. They refuse to take jobs or they quit them, not because jobs are not available, but because at their age level, steady work is not an appropriate response. By the time they reach adulthood—their twenties—and begin to take on family responsibilities, they take on regular jobs, and work becomes a dominant pattern for both whites and blacks. Blacks still have a higher rate of unemployment, but one much lower than for teenagers.

HOROWITZ   Would you like to take over the floor for discussion?

QUESTION   There have been many middle-class youth who have been voluntarily opting for a kind of downward mobility (what you have called a marginal fringe), plus there have been many people from professional or managerial jobs who have been part of the "back to the land" movement. This, again, has constituted a kind of downward mobility.

I am wondering if these fringe elements might in reality be a fringe of the future, not just a marginal fringe of people who cannot make it, and whether also there could not be policies set up that would facilitate this restructuring. One possible policy would be to tax full-time employment more heavily than part-time, or somehow make part-time work more desirable. Also, shouldn't we be considering combining high-status mental work with physical work as a possible alternative? If a person worked part-time in a high status job and also part-time in physical labor, this arrangement would open up a combination of high- and low- status jobs to many more people. What do you think of that type of solution?

HOROWITZ   I appreciate the sobriety of the question. It is really a rhetorical question. I am not going to try to convince you that alternative life-styles should not be

worked out. But if you are talking about the people involved in alternative life-styles, they too have certain characteristics. Those who have accepted downward mobility
tend to be white sons and daughters of an affluent middle
sector. They tend to participate as a special marginal sector of society. I could not agree with you more on the need
to combine head and hand, to combine intellectual and
manual labor. In some measure, that is a characteristic of
the Chinese experiment—if you want to put it into those
terms. There are economies of scale. Not everyone can combine intellectual and manual labor outside their backyards.

There are serious questions about whether you can obtain even minimal levels of growth in an advanced society
by "New Harmony" utopias and the new kinds of communities that are now being advocated: windmill societies, for
example. I have been much impressed by the sincerity and
integrity of the people involved in the development of alternative communities. I have the greatest doubt, however,
that they have developed self-sufficiency or high enough
levels of output to satisfy a consumer-oriented society such
as ours. And I am not entirely sure whether the acceptance
by that sector of the population of the revolution of falling
expectations really alleviates the problem, because they are
not the problem to begin with.

I do not think that young, college-educated people who
decide on alternative life-styles are the core of the dilemma. The core of the dilemma is still characterized by
Herman Miller's data on income distribution in American
society, which throughout the entire twentieth century has
hardly moved a fraction of a percentage point between the
top 10 percent who have, and the bottom 10 percent who
do not. Now there will always be a top 10 percent and a
bottom 10 percent. But the interesting thing in terms of the

available information is the hairline movement between affluent sectors of the society and impoverished sectors. Even when we talk about the gains that women have made, we are still talking about a majority of the population in the labor force who earn 67 percent of what men earn in relation to equivalent job descriptions and opportunities. This is down, not up, from the 1960 census.

While marginality may be the way out for a small cluster of people who are not the core of the problem to begin with, I do not think thay can be the solution to the problem of equity—not in aggregate terms, at any rate. Alternative life-styles are part of an ongoing communalization of life: a search for meaning in terms of the interaction of communities that know one another and that can have impact on the decisions that are taken. And they may have a large-scale impact over time; but, for the most part, I do not think that kind of solution represents any kind of short-run possibility.

QUESTION   Professor Lipset, I would be interested in tying in some of your remarks with the political situation. Specifically, as regards to your recent article entitled "The Paradox of American Politics," you counsel for compromise and for the assertion of claims within the rules of the game rather than by taking a stance of moralistic extremism. It appears to me that your political prognosis foresees increased political repression internally and further international conflict in regard to our foreign policy. Furthermore, I read you as saying in that article that we have it pretty good relative to other countries or the times, and we should keep that in mind. Now, the first question that comes to mind is, how does the international stratification system relate to your diagnosis of the American political system? If politics is to be seen in non-value terms in the sense of this pragmatic keeping to the game as long as the game pays off—and what we are hearing is the game is certainly not going to be paying off for the United States, both internally and internationally—does that mean down the road is repression and violence?

LIPSET   With respect to "The Paradox of American Politics," an article that appeared in the Fall 1976 issue of *The Public Interest,* I would note that I was not advocating compromise, but rather analyzing the way the system works. I stressed two aspects of American politics: moralism, which is expressed often in the many social movements that have characterized our history, and compromise, which is inherent in the unique American party system. New social values often first enter the society as the raison d'etre of moralistic movement politics. These movements force the major parties to move beyond the realm of the normal compromise structure endemic in their being heterogeneous coalitions of diverse interests and factions.

Personally, I think our political system can handle domestic problems, that the tensions of the 1960s do not reflect deep-rooted structural problems. It is less certain, however, that the American political system is up to dealing with international tensions, our relations with the communist world, and, even more difficult, relations with the "South"—the impoverished, massive, less-developed nations. The poorest of them, which are not blessed with oil or other scarce raw materials, are moving backward relative to the developed, middle-level, and oil rich countries. The increase in the cost of oil has hurt them worse than the wealthy nations. For India, the increase in the price of oil has been a disaster. It has meant that they have not been able to buy fertilizers made from petrochemicals, and the increased price of fertilizer has adversely affected Indian food production.

The poor nations, of course, are weak and in no position to conduct wars against the rich countries. But they may be able to conduct a kind of blackmail. The spread of nuclear weaponry may mean that very poor countries will get hold of their own bombs and use them to threaten wealthier countries. A kind of international terrorism may develop seeking to distribute international goods among impoverished countries. The international stratification situation poses difficult problems, ones for which there is no foreseeable solution because the resources to equalize the disparities are simply not there at the moment. It is a great irony that all around the world those who seek to change the situation in underdeveloped and nonindustrial countries operate under the banner of Karl Marx, a theorist of revolution in affluent, highly productive advanced industrial society.

Karl Marx's theory of social change held that socialism could only come about in advanced industrial societies— that a precondition for socialism was a high level of affluence, one that almost eliminated work, that would be produced by capitalism. Political movements in those poor countries that hold power in the name of Marx are in no position to create affluence from domestic resources in a foreseeable period. This fact presses them to attack and blame the wealthy countries, sometimes even the Soviet Union, for their poverty. Will they do something about this? Can they do anything about this? Will we feel morally obligated to try to do something? I do not count very much on the sense of moral obligation, though there is a lot of talk about it. But whether the income gap will increase the incidence of international terrorism, which it may in the long run, is something I think we have to be concerned about.

QUESTION   Would you address yourself more to the internal situation. What would be your understanding of the American political process and how it affects the diminished pie or increases the sense of limited goods that is going to permeate our future in a political context? How do you see that translating into political life?

LIPSET   At the present time I think the issue of growth vs. no growth is becoming a class-related one, as I mentioned earlier. The trade union movement is clearly on the side of maintaining growth, even if the cost of maintaining growth is a polluted environment. Some see the choice as being between pollution and growth. The United States clearly can continue to grow. Most economists believe in the economic law: necessity is the mother of invention, or, if the price is right, someone will supply it. They assume, therefore, that need and demand will produce the increased resources necessary for growth.

QUESTION   By phrasing the conflict as one of jobs vs. cleanliness, you are looking at it from the perspective of the economy as it is now functioning and with a limited perception of what the government is capable of doing under different impetuses. And you are, in a sense, accepting Jackson's definition, not Udall's or that of those who argue that to reorient our economy to one that would be much less polluting would require putting many more people to work, but putting them to work in a context that would probably require them to be paid by the government. Would you respond to that?

HOROWITZ   Even if you reach a point where American society achieves both equity and abundance, you are then faced with all the problems of the world as a whole and what has been called the "Fourth World" in particular. You now have a kind of pattern variable where four alternatives exist. High energy-high food describes the situation in the U.S. and Western Europe, while high energy-low food is found in the Middle East. Low energy-high food countries include Yugoslavia and Eastern Europe. Low energy-low food is characteristic of Bangladesh, the Sahel, and about fifty other countries. These nations, the Fourth World, are defined precisely in terms of the unavailability of either energy resources or food resources. How can you have stability or any kind of rational ordering of a world in which you have that kind of four-part division? So the very successes of American society, presuming they are successes, create dilemmas in other parts of the world.

What are the different responses to the current transformation in theories? One response is that environmentalism combines with a kind of neo-isolationism. If, in fact, you begin to think in terms of community rather than nation; if you think in terms of satisfying immediate food needs or demands for environmental cleanliness, then the more global aspects of political relations necessarily and perforce go by the boards. In part, we have had a kind of middle-class environmental isolationism, which is more of a bane for the present political structure than anything else. As a result, the new middle classes have adopted a posture of privatism, and instead of offering themselves as a model for American civilization as a whole, they have become a strong source of hiding out from the problems of race, religion, and urban decay. The middle classes have now opted out of the very celebration they helped to create.

Even to the extent that you satisfy the thirst and the thrust toward equity within a national domain, that very achievement creates patterns of isolation from the problems of the rest of the world. How this can be coped with within the framework of the national state is itself a complicated problem. Yet we are moving rapidly toward equity as a central item on the political agenda. Otherwise, what does it mean to talk about nuclear blackmail, international terrorism, or military preparedness? I do not have any great optimism, precisely because every scenario I have designed that satisfies and resolves the national picture still leaves unanswered and untapped the entire domain of international relations and foreign affairs. If you cannot have global resolution—and indeed we have now talked quite a bit without even alluding to that global dimension—and instead make the kind of animal faith assumption that there is not a world outside of America, then I can hardly imagine, given present cultural isolationism and present tendencies to look to military solutions as the only available ones, that you are going to have a resolution that, in fact, will be pacific in character.

LIPSET   This is an important point. As you say, it moves us somewhat away from what we have been talking about, because part of the American malaise, the new American view of the world and the international economy, has produced a new isolationism, one related to a sense of hopelessness about the world picture. Our hope-lessness is not in terms of the prospects for peace, because ironically one of the things that may be credited to the atomic stalemate (although it cannot go on forever) is a deterrent strategy that has worked.

We have had a long period of relative international peace; there have been a lot of small wars, but no big world war. Peace, however, is not enough to satisfy Americans. After World War II the United States was op-timistic about the possibility for increased democracy in the world and for sharp improvements in the underdevel-oped countries—a rise in their standards of living, educa-tion, and the like. Our utopian, messianic sense was grati-fied by the belief that we were bringing democracy, peace, and prosperity to the whole world. American universities were full of people working on problems of political and economic development. Thirty years later our interna-tional role is regarded as a disaster.

There are few stable political democracies outside the developed world of Europe, North America, Australia, New Zealand, and Japan. Vietnam, from whatever per-spective anyone had on the war, was a total failure from the American point of view. In this context of hearing about the poverty, the lack of democracy, the other troubles of countries from Bangladesh to Egypt (where the Aswan Dam is a disaster), we seek to withdraw to what some people once wanted to call "fortress America," where we could maintain our own decent society. On the left and the right, among liberals and conservatives, differ-ent variants of the new isolationism have emerged. Stu-dents are less interested in courses dealing with foreign countries. Foreign language learning has declined sharply in the colleges. Trends, fortunately or unfortunately, depending on whether you like the ones we are in at a given moment, have a habit of reversing themselves quickly. It may be this new isolationism will not last very long. But it certainly exists, and its existence serves to increase our ignorance of what is occurring abroad.

QUESTION   Speaking of imminent malaise, maybe we can tie together the discussion on elections with the problem stresses of equality. Professor Lipset has a widely quoted essay on who votes and who does not in which he posits the high turnout person as someone more highly educated, more aware of issues, and so on. We have a situation in recent years in which the number of people being educated has increased tremendously; issues are getting stickier than ever, and yet voter turnout is declining. Some even say that in the upcoming elections, perhaps half or less of those eligible will actually vote. How does this jibe with your earlier discussion of who votes and who does not?

LIPSET   There are two aspects to the question. First, the general point about the correlates of voting still holds. The more educated people are, the more likely they are to vote. The more involved or related their occupational position is to political issues, the more likely they are to vote. It is the deprived—the culturally deprived, the educationally deprived, the organizationally deprived—who vote less. Now, as you are saying, a kind of logic might be suggested that implies that the more education there is, the higher the turnout rate will be over time. But the larger context that determines the proportion voting, the amount of interest from country to country and from time to time, is set by the issues, by the political culture of the moment.

If you study a country like Sweden, where close to 90 percent vote, you find the same correlates. The 10 percent who do not vote in Sweden tend to come from less-educated, poorer people; women vote less than men, young people less than middle-aged people, and so forth. But clearly, a 90 percent vote in Sweden (and bear in mind only 54 percent voted in the United States in the 1976 election) does not, conversely, indicate that the Swedes are better educated or are more affluent than the Americans, but that Swedish political culture is different. Perhaps the choice of candidates is different, perhaps the relations of people to parties and to issues are different. These correlates of voting remain more or less the same from country to country and from time to time, but the nature of the choices and the percent voting vary.

The American situation is even more strikingly anomalous than you mentioned. President Kennedy appointed a commission under Richard Scammon, a well-known political analyst, to look into the reasons why the United States had a lower rate of turnout than most other Western countries. The Scammon Commission concluded that, in large measure, the reasons were technical, that there were greater legal difficulties put in the way of American voters than existed in Britain, Canada, Sweden, Germany, and other places. The then American requirement that people register months before an election, that they register annually, does not exist in the other countries. In Canada and Britain, for example, people are registered whether they want to be or not by a government registration office. All they have to do is decide to vote on the day of the election. The residence requirements in the U.S. are not as stringent elsewhere or do not exist at all.

Looking at this record, the Scammon Commission concluded that if the United States rid itself of these technical restrictions that made it more difficult to vote, then the vote here would move up sharply. Many of the recommendations of the Scammon Commission were implemented either by legislation or by court rule. The residence requirement has largely been eliminated, permanent registration exists in most areas and so forth. Yet, even though many of the Scammon recommendations were carried through, the proportion of the population voting has declined. Political events have proved to outweigh changes in the rules. It is hard to argue that Americans do not vote because of the absence of clear-cut choices. The ideological choices in 1972 were quite distinct between Nixon and McGovern, and yet the voting turnout proportionately was the second lowest in history. Perhaps the choices were too far apart. Many people did not want to choose between the two. In one public opinion poll, conducted by Daniel Yankelovich, the survey did not just ask "Are you for Nixon or McGovern?" but inquired, "Are you for Nixon, McGovern, or neither?" "Neither" won.

There are many hypotheses that could be advanced as to the sources of nonvoting. Perhaps, as Professor Horowitz suggested, many nonvoters are reacting to the realization that whether we elect a Democrat or Republican, 98 percent of what went on before continues. The Republicans promise to cut down government, and they do not; in fact, they increase it. The Democrats promise to expand government, and then they cut back welfare. The very coalition nature of the party system makes the electoral choices less real. Maybe these factors are more important. I do not know. The growing size of American life has produced the grist for a lot of hypotheses.

I should note here, however, the interesting countertendency that certain kinds of citizen participation have increased even as voting participation has decreased. There are many new voluntary public interest associations such as Common Cause, the Urban Coalition, and the Sierra Club; and movements such as women's liberation, black rights, Jewish organizations and various other ethnic-based movements. Each of these is pressing on the system, and collectively these groups are having a greater impact today than groups like these had in the not too distant past. While more organized groups press on the system, speaking in the name of different parts of the population and often having their way to a greater or lesser extent, fewer people vote. This may mean that these organized groups really are not speaking for very many people. On the whole, except for the black and some other less-privileged ethnic groups, these are largely composed of well-educated political activists who seemingly constitute a small but vocal portion of the population.

QUESTION   Professor Horowitz, you gave an example to prove a point on presidential politics, especially presidential coalitions. You mentioned that with Johnson's failure to run in 1968 and Bobby Kennedy's assassination that followed, the power shifted to Nixon, and that is why he won the election over Humphrey. It was a casual reference in those sequences of events, and I wonder if you would clarify the steps of those events that allowed Nixon to win over Humphrey?

LIPSET   Perhaps I can answer that. Professor Horowitz was making the assumption that if Senator Kennedy had not been assassinated he would have secured the Democratic nomination, and in that case he would have beaten Richard Nixon. It would have been a Kennedy/Nixon race rather than a Nixon/Humphrey race, and Kennedy would have been elected. And it was, therefore, the assassination rather than the sentiment in the electorate that led to Nixon's election.

HOROWITZ The exact sequence of events was: first, the New Hampshire primary, with Eugene McCarthy running against Lyndon B. Johnson. Two months later, when McCarthy had knocked Johnson out in the New Hampshire primary, Kennedy officially entered the presidential primaries. The 1968 elections were profoundly influenced by the subsequent assassination of Robert Kennedy because it threw the balance from the McCarthy/Kennedy groups to Humphrey and alienated large numbers of people who were disenchanted by the Democratic party processes under the Johnson administration. I do not think that the Chicago Convention riots would have taken place had it not been for Robert Kennedy's assassination, and Martin Luther King, Jr.'s, five weeks earlier.

But the sequence of events is not as important as the interruption of political legitimacy. We have not had normal politics in America since 1964. John F. Kennedy would assuredly have run for the second term in 1964, so his assassination led to a series of unnatural political situations.

Nor was 1976 normal. The crippled condition of Governor George Wallace certainly played a role in the strength and size of the Carter vote in the primaries that might have been responsive to the Wallace ideology. We do not have purely rational political behavior. The existence of political violence points to some kind of dramaturgical form of history making. We are living in a precarious condition where these kinds of events are important not only in their actual carrying out, but even in their potential of being carried out. Edward Kennedy is at least in part influenced by what he calls family obligations, which can be interpreted to mean that he would be a ready target as a presidential candidate, more so than he is at present as a senator. Thus, even the choice of candidates and nominees is affected by an era of political violence that is not easy to chart or diagram.

LIPSET   We have to close this off now on what seems to be a pessimistic note. Some of you may have seen a story in a newspaper about a class of elementary school youngsters, I believe in Philadelphia, who were asked by the teacher to write about what they would do if they were president. Over half of the children wrote about fears of assassination; they wrote about being killed if they were president. Now when children in a country associate being president with being killed, this is not a very happy political process.

III. PRESIDENCY

LIPSET   The American presidency is in many ways a unique institution. In previous dialogues we discussed some of the characteristics of the coalition party systems derived from the Constitution of the United States, the differences between a presidential and parliamentary democracy. The division of political power between the president and the Congress does not exist in any other Western country. Not only does the U.S. have these two branches of government, but within the executive branch itself the various departments of government have at least two masters in addition to the public. The people within any agency of government—the State Department, the Interior Department, the Labor Department—report to their political supervisors and carry out policy as set by the president, the secretary, the assistant secretary, and on down. They also, however, report to their congressional subcommittees, because they derive their budgets from subcommittees of the House and, to a lesser extent, the Senate. Those subcommittees have chairpersons and members who often retain power much longer than any given cabinet secretary or other executive appointee.

The civil servants in these agencies have to be attuned to the wishes of their congressional subcommittees. They may be summoned as witnesses to testify on behalf of the budget; they may be called to discuss policy issues. Congress expects that they will tell what they know, how they feel, about given issues, even when they disagree with their political supervisors—even when they disagree with the president or the secretary. A situation where the effective government has two masters, the Congress and the executive hierarchy, exists nowhere else. In the late 1940s Herbert Morrison, then deputy leader of the British Labor government, commented that every time he visited the United States and considered how important this country was to the future of the world, he went home sick. Morrison said he could not understand how a government could function with this division of authority; he was also concerned about the openness of government in the United States—that there are no secrets, especially in the foreign policy arena. We, of course, take this for granted. When there are manifest violations of openness, as in the Watergate situation, the American public is outraged. The American norm requires that people at different levels of government should speak freely about what is going on in government, should make records available, and so on.

These norms and practices are much different in Europe—in England, Sweden, or Germany. A British civil servant may not testify before Parliament. He does not give interviews to reporters. He writes memoranda for his political superiors, and his superiors—the ministers—speak out in Parliament, give interviews, and answer questions. The minister takes responsibility. The public never hears directly from or about the civil servants. Confidentiality is taken for granted. In America the president is not master of his house in the same way as the executive is elsewhere. The populist character of the United States is reinforced by this division of labor. Congress, which is close to the people—the House is reelected every two years—takes on the task of trying to find out what is going on inside the executive branch, what alternative policies have been considered, and so forth.

The book I found most insightful on the American presidency is Richard Neustadt's *Presidential Power*. Although written over two decades ago, (Neustadt served in the Truman administration and was a close observer of Roosevelt's) the book makes a number of interesting points about the presidency that are still valid. He stresses how little authority the president has over the bureaucracy. He points out that when the president gives an order with which a given department disagrees, the officials, more often than not, simply ignore the order. Just before leaving office, President Truman commented that Eisenhower will sit in the Oval office and say "Do this. Do that," but he will discover that nothing will happen. Neustadt contends that when a presidential request or a directive from a higher-up is ignored, 98 percent of the time no one hears anything further about it. The president rarely tries to find out whether his order has been carried out. Occasionally, Neustadt says, there is some checking. An order may be given a second time; again it may be ignored, and that will usually be the end of it. Under what conditions can the president have his way against the will of his underlings? Neustadt argues that the president is most likely to have his way when the issue is public, clear-cut, and has a constituency concerned with it. As Hugh Heclo notes in his comprehensive bibliographic report, *Studying the Presidency:* "The major theme to be found in didactic literature on the Presidency is that the President's power is that of persuasion rather than command. His strength does not lie in his purely administrative abilities but in the moral leadership and vision by which he influences others to do what they should be doing anyway."

Most of what goes on in government, however, is not known to those outside. The permanent bureaucracy, therefore, has an enormous amount of the *de facto* power of the presidency, of the executive. As I mentioned earlier, the bureaucracy is, in fact, watched more carefully by the Congress through congressional subcommittees than by the president. To understand the sources of policy in any given area, it is necessary to have some insight into the interests and values of the bureaucracy. Given the tremendous amount of data collected by American social scientists about the bureaucracy, it is surprising how little is known. There are surveys of the attitudes and backgrounds of many groups, but few of government bureaucrats. Inferences about their political values and the allegiances of specific departments may be made, however, from observations of their behavior over time. It is clear that in most cases there is continuity; that is, the shift from one president to another does not produce much change in policy.

Continuity was particularly evident in the Nixon administration. During the first Nixon term, as the Nixon people themselves acknowledged, they were unable to reverse the trends set in previous administrations. These trends were continued in ways totally unanticipated by the White House. Affirmative action programs, for example, were carried through more vigorously than by previous administrations. Although Nixon had pledged to reduce government regulation, the Federal regulations book, as I noted earlier, grew from 20,000 to 60,000 pages between 1969 and 1977.

HOROWITZ When discussing American politics prior to an election, we tend to use different categories than those we use after. When we are talking about how to elect someone, or the basis of electoral procedure, we refer to problems of social class, sectionalism, regionalism, interest formation, and ethnicity, and how all these intersect one another. When we talk about the presidency as an ongoing institutional phenomenon, the elements that presumably go into the decision who should be the president either vanish or are obscured by more immediate phenomena.

The point is simply that the presidency as an ongoing event entails an analysis of the role of the federal bureaucracy in relation to that presidency and, beyond the executive managers, an evaluation of the impact of congressional constraint or judicial restraint. Electoral politics is an activity remote from presidential decision-making processes. This is illustrated by your point about Nixon following through on previous presidential commitments in contradistinction to doing what was expected of him by the special interest constituencies that elected him. Indeed, one theory of Watergate is that Nixon was sent to the wall because of his foreign policy decisions, on China in particular, which gave offence to his most loyal preelection supporters.

Are there inexorable laws and constraints having to do with the nature of the presidency so that no matter who occupies the White House the decision-making process is not directly affected? The point is not so much bureaucratic limitations of presidential power from below, but rather the existence of an entirely different realm of power quite beyond presidential control. It has become a matter of some concern how a president, in a nation of zero growth and with a passion for self-revelation rivaling our earlier passion for secrecy, can exercise large-scale influence, especially in foreign policy matters. If there is a justifiable fear about the American presidency, it is that the popular source of power provides an image of potency that recedes over time as the holder of power comes to terms with structural limitations. Even if one is elected as a populist or a semipopulist like Carter, or as a regionalist, or as an antifederalist like Nixon, decision-making outcomes will ultimately not be much different.

What are the relationships between a constituency model and an operational model? Besides bureaucratic sloth or inertia, what are the sources of social constraint that prevent or stimulate a president to perform or not perform certain acts? This leads to another kind of question concerning the American presidency: is American political life becoming more like its counterpart in Western Europe? With the quasi-impeachment of Nixon (even though Nixon resigned under pressure, his decision to resign basically resulted from an impeachment procedure) has the institution of the American presidency become more like that of the European prime minister? The Senate Watergate hearings demonstrate that even an American president can be removed, certainly a unique development to be studied carefully by students of the American political scene.

This is not to suggest that at the first sign of a domestic crisis—such as the presumed improprieties of a budget director, or a crack in the party consensus concerning the Panama Canal—a president will be removed for cause or will voluntarily resign. The presidency is fought for too long and hard for easy, pouting resignations. But it remains the case that presidential accountability to the commonweal has risen precisely at that stage in American history when presidential ability to deliver on basic pledges, i.e., lower taxes or reduced unemployment, has become ever so much more complex.

At another level, presidential power, while remaining the most important political institution in American life, has become weakened as the interest model of politics has become institutionalized. No longer can a president expect automatic support from labor if he is a Democrat, or from business if he is a Republican. Old coalitions that were once stable and steady have become far shakier as each interest group adopts a bartering and bargaining strategy. Loyalties are traded for results, and since interest politics involves higher levels of expectations, the ability of a president to produce satisfactory results to every group is diminished. The Carter constituency, for example, was forged in the heat of a campaign effort. It is not based on large-scale, near-automatic voting blocs as in earlier periods of American politics such as the New Deal period. It is not simply bureaucratic inertia that poses limits to presidential power, but new foreign and domestic constraints alike.

In the past we have not perceived the presidency as something from which its holder can be compelled to resign. The presidency has become even more tentative a source of power than it has been in the past. It is a more transient phenomenon. In that sense, the character of American democracy has become much more like British democracy. It has become increasingly subject to recall processes preventing any excess of power in an imperial presidency. The Nixon demise was not simply the demise of a person or a regime but an end to a concept of the presidency as inviolable. At that level, we have something that extends far beyond the question of bureaucratic restraint or constraint. In other words, the weaknesses of the presidency are not structural. They are not simply a function of the rise of an executive bureaucratic system that provides necessary initiative for legislative enactment, although the interplay of the two is now crucial. What Richard Neustadt saw as inevitable only a decade ago has now become problematic: rule by executive fiat. Curiously, the emotional investiture in the American presidency continues to increase though the actual power of the office seems to decline. Perhaps this is so because the mass media continues to focus the public eye on the presidency as the maker of major decisions. Thus, the emergence of new structural constraints on executive power has often been overlooked. The expectancy rate goes higher as the ability to fulfill diminishes.

At this point, any single decision has the potential to tear the whole presidency asunder. Take Zaire or Angola. The expectancy was that the president, on a question of foreign affairs, would carry the day. But if he had not convinced the Senate, with the help of his entire staff and departmental apparatus, what effect would that have had on the credibility of this president in relation to other foreign policy decisions? If he cannot deliver on other specific pledges and promises he will be in an inexorable dilemma, one inherent in the presidency itself. This flows from the fact that not only do we use different criteria to evaluate the pre- and postpresidential electoral period, but in the post-Nixon era we use different criteria to measure the strengths and weaknesses of the office itself. I am not suggesting that the presidential system is in peril, but rather that any particular president is in a more perilous position as officeholder in the post-Watergate climate.

LIPSET Differentiating between the constituency and the bureaucratic operational models is very useful. Jimmy Carter, however, came into office with a third model, as Jack Knott and Aaron Wildavsky pointed out in an excellent article published in the second issue of the *Woodrow Wilson Quarterly* (Winter 1977)—the expertise model.

Carter's assumption has been that problems have solutions that may be found by consulting experts. As an engineer, he follows an engineering approach to problem solving; experts are expected to provide answers. Conversely, interest groups that are concerned with advancing their limited, selfish goals should be ignored if possible.

I would like to address the question of the constituency model versus the bureaucratic operational model. Both are necessary to explain different aspects of policy under the presidency. When I said earlier that there was continuity between the Nixon administration and previous ones, I did not intend to suggest that it makes no difference who is the president or which party holds office. It definitely does. For example, the Republican party traditionally has had closer ties with the business community than its rivals. The Democratic party has had closer links to the labor movement. This fact makes a difference in areas that are often not noticed by the public. When the Republicans are in office they dominate the National Labor Relations Board. The decisions of the Board therefore tend to be probusiness; when the Democrats are in, board decisions tend to be prolabor.

There are a variety of other areas where the differences in the constituencies to which each party is obligated and sympathetic affect policy. Sometimes, of course, a political party is more sensitive to the interests of those who are opposed to it, or, better yet, it tends to swing between competing interest groups rather than side with groups that are totally committed. The farm bloc is powerful, in large part, because farmers are more prone than other groups to shift allegiances. To understand the orientation of a given administration, therefore, it is not enough to know the interests or values of the groups behind it. But still, continuity rears its head in many fields. In foreign policy, for example. Secretaries of State Kissinger and Vance have followed different styles. There is, however, little difference in their Middle East, Panama Canal, détente, Strategic Arms Limitation Treaty (SALT) politics. The major outlines of American policy have been similar.

There can be no debate about the weakness of the presidency currently, but one must remember also that we are talking in the shadow of the discussions and concern about the rise of the "imperial presidency," of the great power of the presidency today as compared with the past. The image of the imperial presidency is not wrong, and what gave rise to it has not disappeared. It was, and remains, a valid conception. What remains involved today in the concept of the imperial presidency? For one thing, the number of people working directly for the White House, for the executive branch as distinguished from the cabinet departments, has grown steadily. Every recent president has promised to cut down the size of the executive branch. Nixon promised to do so but wound up increasing it greatly. Carter made a big issue of reducing the White House staff, but according to Dom Bonadede in the *National Journal* of March 4, 1978, the Executive Office of the president has grown "since the beginning of the Carter administration." Although Carter particularly emphasized the need for a decline in the activities of the regulatory agencies, "all ten of the major regulatory agencies have registered personnel increases."

Carter has kept part of his promise to cut by transferring some hundreds of employees to other agencies under his direct control. These agencies together number more than Nixon's White House staff. Nixon's staff, in turn, was larger than the staff under Johnson, and so on down the line. Why this growth in the size of the White House personnel? The answer is simple enough: in the American system, unlike the cabinet systems of most other democratic nations, the president and not the cabinet minister is held personally responsible for major decisions. The president, therefore, must have a staff loyal to him, who will oversee the recommendations of the departments.

In the British system cabinet departments have much more autonomy. The prime minister decides who holds cabinet posts, but he does not dictate policy to most of them. The cabinet as a whole is involved in major policy decisions, but individual ministers also have a great deal of discretion. In the American context, however, most major issues must go to the president. He is his own secretary of state; he is his own secretary of the treasury. How can the president—one individual—react to all the memoranda and the proposals he receives from the myriad of government départments? Obviously, he cannot. What he needs, therefore, is a loyal staff to evaluate the work and proposals of the various departments. Stuart Eizenstat, the president's domestic policy advisor, sees all the relevant materials from Treasury, HEW, Commerce, Labor, as well as others. He must have his own large staff. The National Security Council, under Zbigniew Brzezinski, coordinates foreign policy, and many departments besides State are involved. Most of the cabinet departments deal with aspects of foreign relations.

The White House staff, the Executive Office, in effect becomes a second cabinet composed of the president's people. The departments should be the president's too. After all, he appoints the cabinet members. But the cabinet members become the spokespersons of their departments. Califano heads Health, Education, and Welfare, a department that is larger than many national governments. He, like other ministers, winds up representing his department to the president. To control an already enormous and ever-growing government, Nixon and Carter reacted similarly: they increased the number of the president's people.

When Nixon first took office he held a televised press conference to introduce his cabinet members. He emphasized his campaign commitments to an open administration, to regular cabinet meetings, to a cabinet that would really function as a body and would have authority. We now know what actually happened. The power of the White House staff became enhanced under Haldeman and Ehrlichman, and the conflicts over control are well-documented. Nixon did not want independent cabinet members.

Jimmy Carter has repeated the entire Nixon scenario. He introduced his cabinet members to the public and announced that he would have a real collegial cabinet whose members would have broad authority. Has Carter done so? The answer to the reality of cabinet authority may be found in the story of a person who was much rumored in the press as a candidate for the post of secretary of labor, John Dunlop. He was not appointed secretary, although he was strongly recommended by the AFL-CIO for the job. According to the newspapers, Dunlop was rejected because he was considered to be weak on affirmative action for minorities, and various black and women's groups publicly opposed him. I asked Dunlop what happened, saying, "I see you were done in by the politics of the situation." He replied: "No, that is just not true. Carter never intended to appoint me. He said he always meant to appoint Ray Marshall. I believe him. The reason is fairly simple. Look at the cabinet. They all have one thing in common that does not characterize me." I must confess that I could not think what they had in common, but his explanation was simple. "Not one of them has a constituency of his own, and I do." That is, Dunlop had close ties to the labor movement. The labor movement was pushing for him. Had he been appointed secretary of labor, he would have had the AFL–CIO behind him. If a fight between him and the president had developed, and had Dunlop threatened to resign (as he did in the Ford administration), that would have meant a conflict not just with Dunlop but with the labor movement as well. Vance, Blumenthal, and the rest of the cabinet do not have constituencies. Carter appointed people he can remove tomorrow if they disagree with him, knowing that no one will make a big fuss about it. In other words, he deliberately chose people whose structural situation makes them dependent on him. They are in the cabinet as Carter's people, not as representatives of the various segments of the Democratic coalition.

As Nelson Polsby has noted about Carter's top appointees, they do not "reach into the constituencies of the old, New Deal voting coalition. Where are the representatives of the Irish, the Polish, the Jews, the Italians? The cities? The labor unions? Where, indeed, are the long-time active members of the Democratic Party? Not wholly absent, to be sure. But hard to find."

The one exception to this generalization is Andrew Young, who does have a constituency in the black civil rights movement. If Carter were to remove Young as United Nations Ambassador there would be an outcry from blacks. But the black representative is not in an area of direct concern to his constituency. It would seem that Carter deliberately planned to have a weak cabinet, *not* an independent cabinet, and one over which the people in the White House staff can have influence and power. Carter wants to be a strong president. To be a strong president requires that the White House, rather than the cabinet and departments, be the central focus of policy.

A Washington journalist told me recently that soon after the election one of Carter's close advisors, when asked off-the-record whom Carter people had in mind for secretary of state, said, "we are looking for another [William P.] Rogers." Rogers, of course, was Nixon's nonentity secretary of state. With all due respect to Secretary Vance, Carter has found his Rogers, his Rusk. Vance appears to be a decent man, but he is not a strong man. He has not been a strong secretary, and that is not an accident. A weak secretary is the way the President can keep control of foreign affairs. Henry Kissinger, of course, was a strong secretary, but Kissinger's power was built on Watergate, on the weakening of the Nixon presidency.

In spite of his having a strong, loyal White House staff, the president is up against the fact, as Neustadt pointed out, that his span of control is terribly limited. To get things done, Carter has to pick a few issues that are really of concern to him, a few goals that he wants to achieve, and then push on those and forget about the rest. In practice, however, Carter appears to fight on too many fronts, to propose solutions to all problems, foreign and domestic.

If Jimmy Carter has any domestic priority it appears to be government reorganization and increased efficiency. The Wildavsky article referred to earlier, which was written before the election and is based on an analysis of Carter's campaign speeches and his record and statements in Georgia, anticipated this. Wildavsky wrote that Carter has a passion for methods. He wants government to operate effectively. He believes that if he can make it operate efficiently it will operate well and take on all policy issues. Polsby, commenting on Carter's first half-year in the presidency, noted that Carter "has emphasized the importance of design in the making and presentation of public policy, and has deemphasized content. The goals President Carter has stessed are essentially administrative in character: simplification, reduction of duplication, uniformity, predictability, and the establishment of long-term goals. He is a believer in comprehensive reform, in finding once-and-for-all solutions to problems." But as Richard Neustadt has commented in reaction to the argument that Carter's reorganization plans constitute "a Presidential statement": "Procedure is no substitute for judgment."

Yet on the formal organizational level, Carter's proposals for a more efficient government are not that original. Continuity, dictated by the logic of size and tasks, is present here also. As two political scientists, John Helmer and Louis Maisel, noted at the 1977 meetings of the American Political Science Association, "the rhetoric of Executive Office reorganization has remained much the same over the years, and veteran White House advisers and staff write or talk of much the same problems of the policymaking process. A recent review of Executive Office reorganization plans since 1936 concluded that 'there are no new ideas which today's reorganization teams have uncovered which those of the past have not clearly identified or experimented with.' "

The growth of the president's staff has to be seen in the context of the continued expansion of government at all levels. The tasks handled by Congress have multiplied enormously. As Steven Roberts pointed out in *The New*

York Times of March 27, 1978: "The growth of the Congressional work load can be measured by a few facts. About 100 recorded votes were taken in each session 15 years ago, as against 700 last year. In an 11-hour day, a Congressional committee reported last year, the average member has only 11 minutes free to think. For more than one-third of that day, the Representative is scheduled to be in at least two places at once." The problems handled by Congress have become much more technical. For example, "environmental issues require detailed knowledge of chemistry and biology, tax policy and corporate economics."

As a result, congressional staffs have increased greatly. There are many professionals who earn high salaries. Congress now has its own budget office. Congressmen do not simply have to react to the president's budget; they have an excellent economist, Alice Rivlin, who is head of the Congressional Budget Office. She has a staff that makes independent analyses of budgetary needs. There is now a sizable Congressional bureaucracy. Edward Banfield has reported: "Congress now employs some 28,000 professionals, a significant and increasing proportion of whom are trained to do policy-related social science research or analysis. Some of these are employed by individual members and others by committee staffs; [others] are in one or another of severally recently established bodies: The Congressional Research Service (1970), the Office of Technology Assessment (1972), The General Accounting Office's division for program evaluation (1974), and the Congressional Budget Office (1974). There is now serious talk of creating an additional body—an Institute for Congress—to be . . . staffed by professionals 'whose stature and ability would earn the deference of the members.' " Little wonder that one senator, Robert Morgan, stresses that "this country is basically run by the legislative staffs of the Senate and members of the House of Representatives . . . they are the ones who give us advice as to how to vote, and then we vote on their recommendations."

The reasons for this development are that, on a smaller scale, representatives and senators face the same problems that produced the imperial White House. A congressman cannot handle all the issues that come up. As Senator Morgan notes, they must rely on their staff. Of course, when a congressman selects aides, he picks them in part because they agree with him. They have similar ideological orientations. They interact with him; he knows their opinions, and they know his views. There is a feeling of mutual trust. If he is liberal, he is likely to have a liberal staff; if conservative, he has conservative aides.

The lobbyists on the Hill know this. The people they try to educate, to whom they send memoranda, are the staff people because it is these staff people who have specific policy assignments. They are not generalists the way the congressmen must be. The need for specialists is a structural weakness, because the government must have a central or coordinating policy. But since individuals cannot deal with more than a limited amount of the system, specialists have great power. They can impress their superiors; they can confuse their congressmen with details. A congressman who chooses a particular area he knows well and ignores most of the others can, as a result, have considerable influence and power in that area.

Senator Jackson is an example of the power of specialization. He has a great deal of influence in the defense and energy fields. Why does Jackson have this influence? In part, of course, it is a result of seniority; he has been around for a long time and knows many people. But Jackson has developed enormous expertise in these areas. He is a very serious and hardworking man. He goes to seminars; he reads books; he listens to the experts. When he talks to most of his colleagues, they cannot answer him, for they do not know the area as well as he does. He can outtalk and outargue them. As the system grows in size and complexity, it inevitably becomes more differentiated, and power goes to the expert.

From one perspective, government appears imperial because it has grown so large. As a system, the presidency and the government have become all-powerful institutions. But the main consequence of bigness is a high degree of differentiation. And differentiation means that the central corps loses some of its ability to control the system. Perhaps government faces the problem of the dinosaur whose brain could not control its body. Much of the "body" of government goes on with very few signals from the brain. Yet presidents coming into office usually do not appreciate this. Most presidents assume that because they are smart they will know what to do, how to control. But after a while they recognize that this is impossible. Franklin Roosevelt noted in 1939 about a much smaller presidency: "It has become physically impossible for one man to see so many persons, to receive reports directly from them and to attempt to advise them on their own problems which they submit."

Trying to deal with bureaucratic differentiation, the Nixon presidency ended up simply separating itself from the entire problem. The isolation of the Oval Office was, to a considerable degree, a function of Nixon's personality, his shyness and consequent passion for privacy, and his paranoia—his suspicion that the bureaucrats were trying to do him in (as in fact many were). But, independent of personality, the effort to control a differentiated structure means that the president has to be isolated from contact with many people who have good reasons to see him, simply because he is only one person who has only twenty-four hours a day.

Given these developments in the presidency, it is curious that Carter, alone among modern presidents, has tried to operate without a chief of staff with authority to control the flow of information to him and to influence his personal agenda. Carter's White House is organized more like "the spokes of a wheel," with different aides having equal rights of access to him, rather than as a hierarchical structure. Carter is his own chief of staff. Richard Cheney, Gerald Ford's chief of staff, notes critically that this procedure cannot work. "Somebody has to be in charge. Without an orderly structure, there's no accountability, no orderly flow. You always run the risk of being blind-sided." James Howe, Jr., one of Roosevelt's administrative assistants and an adviser to other Democratic presidents as well, agrees: "Carter's doing an awful lot of stuff he shouldn't be doing. He must be exhausting himself on things that aren't that important."

Yet it must be noted that bringing in more generalists, more advisors to the president to whom persons with specialized authority report, cannot eliminate the growing power of the specialists, of those with a comprehensive knowledge of a field. Consider the role of the National Security Advisor. Brzezinski sees Carter every day, submitting many memoranda. He clearly has a great deal of influence. But he, in turn, must react to the Middle East; to Latin America; to the Panama Canal; to the SALT agreement; to international trade negotiations; and to relations with China, Japan, Korea, South Africa, and the Soviet Union.

How does he cope with such an awesome number of duties? He relies on papers prepared by his experts on the Middle East, or on Japan, or on other matters. While he, like the president, may have strong personal views and may override his staff, the views of the experts are crucial. The power of the specialist inherently grows with the increased magnitude of government, while the ability of outside people to influence government declines.

Franklin Roosevelt tried to increase his ability to make the effective decisions by including in his government people with diverse approaches to the same area. Recognizing that different values, interests, and backgrounds produced different "solutions," he deliberately assigned the same problem to different people or agencies with varying biases on the assumption that when they disagreed they would each submit their respective arguments for the alternative strategies to him. Other Presidents followed the same strategy. Under Nixon and Ford, Fred Iklé, the head of the Arms Control and Disarmament Agency, frequently disagreed with Henry Kissinger on arms control issues raised in the SALT negotiations. On one occasion he went to Gerald Ford with his objections to agreements reached by Kissinger with the Russians, and the president overruled the secretary of state.

Carter, however, with his reliance on experts and his insistence that he make all decisions, has effectively reduced his options and has made himself a servant of his subordinates. In the foreign policy-defense field he draws his advice from experts who have been drawn from one ideological camp, New Politics McGovern liberals or members of past administrations who have publicly recanted their roles in Vietnam. In the Transition Task Force, which they dominated, they recommended each other as appointees. The State Department under Carter and Vance is more openly politicized than in recent previous administrations. Neal Boyer, a foreign service officer, noted in a (leaked) confidential memorandum that "of the 36 most senior positions in this department, 22 are now filled by political appointees, as compared with only 12 in the last administration." The orientation of the group may be seen in the comment by George McGovern that State Department appointments have been "excellent . . . quite close to those I would have made myself."

The effect of having almost all foreign policy experts drawn from one ideological camp may be seen in Middle East policy. All those within the administration concerned with the area share the viewpoint outlined in a series of articles by Brzezinski published in 1974 and 1976. The major elements of the Democratic party who disagree with it have been excluded from participation in the discussions within the National Security Council and the State Department.

The prevalence of New Politics supporters in foreign policy and arms control posts, people who are convinced that a mutually advantageous accommodation with the Soviet Union is possible, increasingly worries America's allies in Western Europe and Japan; they see Russian armament policies and maneuvers in the Middle East and Africa as evidence that the Soviets continue to be expansionist. Commitment to withdrawal of U.S. troops in Korea has led conservative Japanese politicians to feel they may have to come to a closer accommodation with their Communist neighbors. European leaders, according to Flora Lewis, writing in the *New York Times* of April 1, 1978, expressed "uneasiness and bewilderment" over Carter's foreign policy. In France, not surprisingly, the conservative paper, *Figaro,* some time ago wrote of its concern over the influence of left-oriented *"progressistes"* on American policy in Europe. But recently, according to Miss Lewis, a "surprising attack came in a front-page article in *Le Monde,* a [left-oriented] newspaper that had long been sharply critical of what it considered over-assertive American 'superpower' attitudes around the world. Now, it said, Washington is failing to protect Western interests, especially in the Horn of Africa, but also in East-West relations generally."

Unlike Franklin Roosevelt, who welcomed conflict and tension within his administration, who gave the various segments of his coalition the sense that their representatives were part of the government even though they obviously could not always have their way, Jimmy Carter sees harmony as a virtue. When asked by Saul Pett of the *New York Times:* "What has been your greatest single satisfaction with the job so far?" Carter replied that it was putting together a "harmonious and highly efficient team."* The way in which Carter's most important domestic program, his energy package, was put together is an example of this emphasis on expertise and harmony. According to the *New York Times,* "the plan was conceived in secrecy by technicians" and "reflected a detached, almost apolitical attitude." Those involved "functioned as if they were a self-contained unit and their task as hush-hush as the Manhattan project." It is hardly surprising, therefore, that those in disagreement with aspects of these policies felt it necessary to wage bitter campaigns to change them.

Since conflicting perspectives are not well represented within the administration, critics of any given policy concentrate their efforts to affect policy on Congress, which does contain major spokespersons for alternative approaches.

New York Times, 23 October 1977, p. 36.

HOROWITZ   The power of the specialist is even reflected in a changing attitude toward words. The word "bureaucracy" had a bad political connotation up to and through the New Deal and Fair Deal periods. Now there is even a journal called *The Bureaucrat*. The term "bureaucrat" has become a label of approbation rather than approbrium. In part, the new sentiment derives from new circumstances. Presidential cronyism has declined; department heads and bureau chiefs are selected for their levels of technical competence. And in this regard, Carter has simply accelerated this shift from party payoffs to political expertise as the basis of loyalty and support. What you have described as a third, or expertise model is simply an extension of Weber's rationalistic model of authority. What you call an expert is a person of knowledge, and a person of knowledge gives information to leadership; the leadership then has to accept or reject that information as a basis of action. What happens is that we talk differently about the presidential process than we do the democratic process because the former has become so profoundly elitist while the latter remained essentially democratic. We are stopped after that exposition, once again at the same dilemma: namely, the process by which one becomes a president is considerably different than the functional activities of the presidency. It is the difference between not only Platonic and Lockian theories, but also between who, in effect, underwrites this gigantic federal superstructure and what it is they are underwriting.

Take the matter of government reorganization dealt with in Wildavsky's essay, which, though brilliant, basically extrapolates from the career of Carter as governor of Georgia. Wildavsky says that you can expect the same approach from Carter in terms of presidential performance. But the net effect on the federal bureaucracy is another story. Although Carter may start by appointing a person in charge of government reorganization who threatens this vast bureaucracy—like Lance, for example—when this person is himself put under pressure, as was Lance, all his time will thereafter be taken up with answering charges about his own behavior. He cannot possibly go about the government reorganization that presumably underwrites the antibureaucratic persuasions of the current president. The magnitude of the reorganization of the government, even of the White House staff, is much larger, and its qualitative nature is inexorably altered as its size and design change. You cannot simply extrapolate from performance at the gubernatorial level to the presidential level. One might argue that this, in fact, is a weakness of the Carter presidency. This is a presidency of outsiders; as a result, they presumed a political world that began with the inauguration of the new chief on January 20, 1977. They further presume that what can be done at the level of Georgia can easily be translated to the federal level. That was a dangerous presumption and one that has not proven itself valid. Government reorganization has not taken place, nor will it take place at anywhere near the magnitude we were promised prior to the election. What has been done, in part, is subterfuge; namely, reorganization by reassignment or relabeling rather than any real reduction in the size of the bureaucratic class or the bureaucracies involved.

Wildavsky's article, while sensitive, missed another element of the Carter position. That is what I would call the petit-bourgeois nature of the Carter ideology. I want to be specific about this so that we do not get into a debate about Marxism—vulgar or sophisticated. Carter's entire ideological framework is characterized by a revulsion for bigness—big business, big labor, and even the big government bureaucracy he seems incapable of reducing. What Carter really likes is the idea of an abstraction known as "John Q.

Public" fighting back with little business and little labor. It is the idea of work, but not the idea of a working class; the idea of commerce, but not the idea of multinationals that appeals to him. His whole conception of the world is rooted in the small business background whence he emanated.

In part, this is revealed by his attitudes toward land redistribution in the West, in which he wants to bring about a situation where those who till the land own it. He would like to curtail sharply the power of the large oil companies. This notion flies in the face of economies of scale. Size is conceded to have no bearing on effective farm management or petroleum discoveries—nothing to do with the cost of equipment to bring about higher crop yields or great natural gas deposits. None of the standard arguments supporting the contributions of size to development prevail for Carter. What prevails is a concept of the toiler, the tiller, the small entrepreneur; the belief that the person who works should be rewarded. The person who works on the land does not need agribusiness executives. Likewise, the studied disregard of the Carter administration for the AFL-CIO positions has to do not with any special animus toward George Meany or any antipathy toward union precepts, but with the feeling that big unions are bad simply because they are big, just as big business is evil because it is big. Bigness worries this administration; on the other hand, it is bigness that it does not know how to cope with or get beyond.

Another side of this coin is the marriage of petit-bourgeois conscience to Christian faith, which fosters the entirely negative attitude toward the potential for corruption wherever power is concentrated. One might argue that this element was crucial in Carter's electoral appeal by allowing him to maintain the spectre of Nixon without having to attack the disgraced president and risk a possible accusation of conducting a smear campaign, which might have had a boomerang effect. But the assault on corruption too easily spills over into a requirement for moralist posturing that can weaken, if not cripple, key government agencies and, worse, frighten those expertise elements from federal participation that Carter is relying upon to reduce the swollen bureaucracy.

If the line between political vice and virtue is drawn with absolute certainty, instead of the best and the brightest, the executive may end up with the slothful and the sluggish. The line between perquisites and graft has purposely been left vague for politicians who serve. To remove such ambiguity, to rigidify moral standards, is to make suspect everyone in government service who drives a Cadillac rather than a Chevrolet. It may also have the effect of increasing the size of the bureaucracy by increasing legislative and executive demands for more staff personnel and payments to keep pace with private industry rewards. The petite bourgeoisie believes in economic honesty because it has traditionally discounted the value of its own labor power. But whether such a sense of sacrifice can transcend rumors and removals in the present climate of Washington is hard to foretell.

Carter reveals a peculiar class problem. We witness the elevation of the petite bourgeoisie to the presidency in an era of growing oligopolistic concentration in the hands of big business. Whatever you want to call it—multinational business; monopolistic tendencies; unharnessed, big, centrally organized labor in terms of one giant umbrella organization with maybe the Teamsters as an adjacent organization—all of this has proven confounding to a president who believes in town meetings and town houses, anything rather than big labor and big business. One of the fascinating aspects of this president's ideology is the manner and extent to which he responds to and resonates with the needs of little people, as exemplified by telephone marathons and town hall meetings. His responsiveness to women, blacks, and other minorities is authentic. Besides his seeing in those groups elements of American society who traditionally have been deprived of their fair share, he sees also large numbers of people who seem to agree with him that small is beautiful. One cannot disregard the fact that Carter does share in the ecological tenet that "small is beautiful." I do not mean in terms of zero growth necessarily, but in terms of little people who are the moral athletes of American society. For Carter, neither big business nor big labor can be the moral savior of U.S. society. The savior turns out to be all of those outsider elements that fused around the Carter candidacy. The trouble is that electoral fusion is no sign of postelectoral consensus. And the growing dismay with Carter for failing to deliver is indicative of this sad truth.

Carter believes that there is a whole constituency that can somehow be serviced by the Democratic party other than the traditional, big labor base of the party. You have a peculiar nineteenth-century ideology married to a dramatic twentieth-century rise of marginal sectors in American society, of nonproletarian, nonbourgeois sectors of society—what Daniel Bell speaks of as the expanding sector in American society. Carter conceptually organized those marginals, whether they were blacks or poor farmers, into an electoral and even ideological coalition. But it has had trouble surviving its own election victory. Some kind of class reorientation is going on, and we should not simply view this in administrative terms, or in terms of a president who is locked into a bureaucratic process from whence he cannot escape. He does give voice to new formations, to social formations that are the basis of his support, and, at the same time, the source of his weakness as well. This affinity for a small entrepreneurial ideal, for instance, is not one that is easily shared by welfare mothers or urban workers.

LIPSET   I agree with you. Some time ago in a discussion, a long-term former Democratic congressman still living in Washington described the Carter administration as a "New Politics" one. He said this in the context of explaining why so many New Politics people who had not been pro-Carter from the beginning hold important posts throughout the Carter administration. The administration, particularly in subcabinet appointments, has a large number of strong McGovern supporters, many of whom backed Fred Harris and Mo Udall for the nomination, while almost no one who supported Henry Jackson holds a major position. A *Fortune* writer, Juan Cameron, writing in the October 1977 issue of the magazine, documents in detail the fact that "a great many of the sub–Cabinet-level positions have been given to a diverse array of public-interest lawyers, consumerists, civil-rights workers, and environmental advocates." The former congressman contended that even though Carter may not have known the ideological backgrounds of any particular individual and did not directly appoint most of them, these people are there because they represent tendencies and approaches to government that are in tune with his own. As an antiestablishment outsider, he prefers others like himself. Cameron notes in a similar vein that "there is no question that a curious affinity exists between the Georgian's traditional populism and the leftist thinking of the public-interest people who surround him."

The reliance on New Politics supporters does not contradict Carter's dependency on expertise, his concern with finding the correct "solution" to problems. He finds his experts among New Politics academics and public service, public-interest lawyers. In so doing, ironically, he follows in the footsteps of Richard Nixon who also depended on lawyers, albeit corporate ones, and professors. The record of recent administrations suggests that the increasing complexity of issues has produced a shift from businessmen and politicians to experts. If Eisenhower's cabinet could be described as nine millionaires and a plumber (the secretary of labor), the Nixon-Ford and Carter administrations may be called governments of professors.

The first professors' government known to history held office for a few weeks in Vienna during the Revolution of 1848. More recently a government of professors held office under Nixon and Ford, although nobody seems to have noticed. There was Professor Kissinger at National Security and the State Department; Professor Schultz at Treasury; Professor Schlesinger at the CIA and Defense; Dean Butz, former professor, in Agriculture; Professor Moynihan in Domestic Affairs; Professor Levi in the Attorney General's office; Professor Dunlop in Labor; Professor Matthews at HEW; and Professor Burns at the Federal Reserve Bank. The latter appointment is especially noteworthy, since the Federal Reserve Bank has traditionally been headed by bankers. Marriner Eccles, who chaired the Federal Reserve Bank under Roosevelt, was a banker, not a professor. Nothing in that interesting television serial drawn from the experiences of the Nixon administration, *Inside Washington,* was more misleading than the statement of President Monkton (Nixon), one that Nixon actually made: "Don't hire anyone from Harvard." Nixon's administration was full of people from Harvard and other

Ivy League schools. Nixon obviously did not appoint academics because as a group they were Republicans, or conservatives, or because he had a constituency in academe. He appointed them because they were experts who presumably knew their fields.

Carter, as noted, is doing the same thing, although he has more people with Washington bureaucratic experience in his cabinet than did Nixon and Ford, with academic authorities concentrated at the subcabinet level. Still, there are many academics at the summits of Carter departments: Brzezinski at National Security; Brown at Defense; Marshall at Labor; Schlesinger at Energy; and Kreps at Commerce. Blumenthal at Treasury is a businessman, but he is a businessman with a Ph.D. degree who is a former professor and who does not have strong ties to the business community. He resembles McNamara, Kennedy's and Johnson's secretary of defense, another businessman who was an ex-professor and who retained close relations to the academic world. As president of the Ford Motor Company, he lived in Ann Arbor, rather than in one of the Detroit suburbs preferred by automobile executives.

The increased power of the mandarins within government is a consequence of the emphasis on expertise, all of which reflects the emergence of a postindustrial, knowledge-based society in which the research and development sector, whose summits are the universities and think tanks, plays a major role. This complex system can be run only by people who have dedicated their lives to being authorities in a particular area.

A third major characteristic of the leadership of the Carter administration, particularly of the White House staff, is that it is composed of outsiders. Except for Brzezinski, the top echelon are all Georgians. Georgians, as such, are no better or worse than the Boston Irish mafia that Kennedy had, or the California mafia that surrounded Nixon, but a Georgian background is inherently more provincial. Los Angeles, Cambridge, and Boston are more within the mainstream of knowledge and action than Atlanta. The people who entered the White House with Carter knew each other well in Georgia and interacted throughout his long campaign. Given the isolation of the White House, staffing it with Georgians will not broaden those within it. Being at the summit, they have, of course, been able to meet everybody in Washington and thus become more cosmopolitan, but they still remain a clique who basically rely on each other. The information they most readily accept comes from people like themselves.

In an article published a year after Carter's election, the London *Economist* noted:

it is now clear that Mr. Carter's most vaunted asset—the fact that he was a political outsider, free from evil ways—is his greatest liability. . . . His White House staff, dominated by a tight-knit group of Georgians under no clear chief, has presented an unfortunate mix of high-handedness and innocence to the world. Decisions are reached, and then altered, with a minimum of consultation. Unlike Mr. Nixon's henchmen in many good ways, these young men share one dangerous quality: they regard Washington as the enemy.

A provincial outsider group has taken over the White House. Carter balanced them, I am sure, consciously, by appointing many Washington insiders to the cabinet, a fact that shocked his Georgian populist collaborators. It may be recalled that Hamilton Jordan said that "if you find Vance and Brzezinski in this administration, you'll know we did something wrong." These two and others like them were appointed, but Jordan and his friends are there to control them.

The White House outsiders are there to give the president his options, to protect him against the departments. They are supposed to manage the Califanos, the Browns, the Harrises, and the Blumenthals. Outsiders in the White House, insiders in the cabinet, and New Politics experts at the middle levels characterize this administration.

Carter's conception of government is a populist one. As a populist, he does not like interest groups. It is clear that he believes interests are bad, selfish, and have a narrow conception of the public interest. Labor defends labor, business defends business. The government should represent all the people. What is wrong with this view is that it is basically apolitical and undemocratic. Populism does not recognize that democracy is inherently pluralistic, that it is based on conflict among interests, that coalitions among diverse interest groups are the stuff of politics, that there is no common interest other than that which emerges out of struggle, compromises, and, if you will, deals. In his rejection of interests, as Wildavsky mentions, Carter resembles the unlamented former politician John Lindsay. When Lindsay became mayor of New York, he announced he would not deal with the "power brokers." He would not negotiate private deals with the unions. On January 1, 1966—the day he took office—the unions went on strike. His predecessor, Robert Wagner, had made covert agreements with the unions and actually negotiated better contracts from the city's point of view than Lindsay did subsequently. Lindsay, who tried to represent the people against the interests, was broken by these interests and actually gave into them more than the wheelers and dealers did.

Carter took office with a similar perspective. He, too, was determined not to deal with the interest groups. He would represent the interests of the people. But what happened? The interests revealed their power. When various of them began to manifest anger at being ignored, Carter quickly backtracked. Carter is a man who, like Nixon, was elected by a narrow electoral college majority and who, as a consequence, began to work on his reelection campaign from the day he entered office. The famous Pat Caddell memo submitted to him at the beginning of the administration outlined a strategy for reelection: go on television, have frequent press conferences, visit people in their homes, speak at town meetings—advice that he has followed. To be reelected, he must have the votes, and, in particular, he must not alienate the constituencies that elected him.

A pattern of standing on high principle and then capitulating to the interests emerged in the first year of the Carter presidency, which was to continue. After refusing to deal with the AFL-CIO for some time, he suddenly shifted and began to strongly espouse positions on minimum wage and trade union rights legislation, which the union movement advocated. The AFL-CIO had become publicly angry with him. Its leaders expressed regret about their role in backing him in 1976. George Meany voiced regret for having worked so hard for Carter in 1976, threatened not to repeat his support in 1980, and eventually Carter gave in. After opposing organized farmer demands for further land diversion that would raise prices to the consumer, the president, on March 29, 1978, proposed to increase payments to farmers who cut back in planting, or agreed not to harvest crops already planted. Shortly after taking office, Jimmy Carter attacked the "pork barrel" approach to approval of water projects and announced that many unnecessary ones should be cancelled. By the Spring of 1978, he was under attack by the Coalition for

Water Project Review, a coalition of twenty-six conservation groups, for making "one concession after another" to special interests in this field.

Similar phenomena occurred with respect to foreign policy. Carter and Brzezinski basically believe in a policy of pressing Israel to compromise, to yield on crucial issues in order to gain peace, particularly with respect to the demands of the Palestinians, compromises which Israel regards as against its security interests. Pressure by the U.S. on Israel has repeatedly created a conflict between Carter and pro-Israel groups, particularly the Jews but others as well, most of whom have been traditional Democrats. As these groups reacted with strong attacks on the administration, the White House tended to back down. After one such confrontation in July 1977, Carter held a meeting with the presidents of major Jewish organizations at which he said that, unlike his predecessor, the U.S. would never put pressure on Israel by threatening to withhold aid, that they may disagree, but that such disagreements are disagreements among close friends. In October, following strong public expressions of outrage against the joint U.S.-Soviet statement calling on Israel to recognize "the legitimate rights of the Palestinians" (and on the Arabs to accept Israel as a legitimate state, entitled to security guarantees), Carter gave in again. He told a group of pro-Israeli congressmen that he would sooner commit "political suicide" than endanger Israel's security. By the spring of 1978, the difficulties in the Egyptian-Israel peace negotiations finally led the administration to engage in a public confrontation with Israel, insisting that the Begin government be more flexible with regard to yielding land in the West Bank, and proposing arms aid to Egypt and Saudi Arabia.

The pattern of public confrontation and retreat under pressure has occurred repeatedly. Such shifts reduce Carter's credibility among all those involved in the conflicts at home and among our friends and enemies abroad. By the end of Carter's first year in office, he had become increasingly subject to critiques that closely resembled those directed against John Lindsay. *Newsweek* was to report: "The complaint is commonplace in Washington that Carter, far from being the stiff-necked purist of Georgia legend, bends too easily under pressure," while an article in the *New York Times* commented: "Once perceived as being 'too stubborn,' Mr. Carter is now seen by many as a man prone to retreat too quickly." The *Economist* suggested that the behavior of the White House has "made our conclusion of a year ago seem almost embarrassingly prophetic: 'Mr. Carter has shown an alarmingly visceral streak when under pressure.'"

The populist view of politics is unrealistic. A conception of a politics that does not involve conflict and compromise among interests is naive. Like Lindsay, Carter has turned out to be more vulnerable to interest-group pressure than politicians who recognize that they have to negotiate with interests to maintain an effective coalition. Carter, it should be noted, is not alone in his populism these days. Congress contains a large group, referred to by veteran congressmen who have little respect for them, as "the Watergate group," Democratic congressmen elected in 1974 and 1976 as a result of the scandal. These congressmen are largely young New Politics and antiwar idealists, who consider themselves liberals. They look upon older congressmen, the people who have been there before them, as politicians. They think of themselves not as politicians, but as idealists representing the interests of the people. Like Carter, they are not going to compromise with interests; but, like him, they have to take into consideration the problem of getting reelected. They think of themselves as being to the left of the Democratic party, and dislike many groups within it. They oppose the labor movement; they do not like George Meany. They initially voted against the legislation requested by labor, but then gave in to pressure and voted for it. Their overall record is more conservative than that of older Democratic congressmen, for they yield to pressure more easily. They are really Carter's people even though they may not think of themselves as Carterites. The outsider antiestablishment New Politics self-image held by the president and many of these congressmen produce comparable orientations even though they were not previously allied.

To return to the general issue of the weakness of the Carter presidency, it is worth noting that a large part of it may be related to certain basic trends in democratic politics, specifically, the fact that welfare states are exposed to steadily increasing demands from growing numbers of well-organized, mobilized issue groups. Governments are under pressure to satisfy the often contradictory demands from these constituencies. The sheer capacity of politicians to satisfy the pressures on them has declined. Thus, as the various publics have been educated to demand more from their governors, those in office find it impossible to deal with them. New York City broke down financially. On a large scale, the U.S. government faces the same dilemma. Those at the summits, mayors and presidents, are blamed for their failure to respond. Not surprisingly, therefore, their popularity goes down. Ironically, the very growth of government and increase in the size of the presidency make them appear weaker, ineffective.

HOROWITZ   Let me change the level of the discussion to one of ideology rather than organization. We have in the Carter administration two concepts of running the government, or of being president. One is an engineering concept, and the other is a religious concept. On one hand we have probably the least morally oriented point of view possible: namely, the engineering model, in which the president organizes his regime in terms of balancing interests—creating a kind of stasis, maintaining equilibrium, adjudicating problems whenever and wherever possible, never taking a stand on the basis of right and wrong, left or right, Democrat or Republican, but always on the basis of balancing various competing parts. This is evident, for example, in the Middle East policy of Carter. He is pro-Palestinian and pro-Israeli. He believes Palestinians should have a voice and a place at the negotiating table. He believes that Israel has a right to exist and to survive as a state within the Middle East. He says nothing that would fuel moral outrage insofar as he can help it; and yet, he can offer little in the way of political activity that is effective in an atmosphere of inherited animosities and quick tempers, such as is often found in real political battles.

Such ambiguity would be satisfactory if we could pin Carter down as having an engineering ideology. We would at least know what to expect. But, in point of fact, underwriting his engineering ideology is a higher theology in which there is a presumed moral basis to political behavior. What has led to an enormous amount of confusion in writing about Carter, and in writing about the first year of his presidency, is a tendency to focus either on his engineering qualities or his religious qualities and to try to characterize him in those terms alone. Carter is both an engineer and a religious man. And why not? Do not engineers go to church on Sunday morning? Is it not the case that engineers are often the most conservative in terms of political practice and orientation? Are they not traditionally a group that believes heavily in a morally based politics? Complex techniques and simplistic morals often go together in American political history; and now in the American presidency.

We are dealing with a peculiar contradiction that cannot be resolved because Carter has not yet come upon a crisis situation where he must make a decision solely on the basis of either an engineering model or a Christian model of ethical persuasion. We should not forget that we are dealing with an administration less than one year old. We are, furthermore, making assumptions about crisis events that have not yet happened. The real test of whether we are dealing with an engineer or a moralist will be a crisis that he cannot evade or avoid, and one he cannot contain, and thus one he must respond to. That crisis may be South Africa, Panama Canal ownership, the Middle East, or the SALT negotiations. The test of this particular presidency will come at that moment in time when the choice is either to compromise, as any good engineer should, or to engage in a battle of principle as a good Christian. The frequent references to the Wilson presidency are understandable: pacifist and militarist stand in uneasy alliance and even with a World War behind him, Wilson never quite made up his mind what set of "principles" was central, those of American hegemony or those of an American-led effort at world disarmament.

My understanding of this particular presidency is that Carter's contradiction resides in an inability, perhaps a psychological inability, to resolve these two components that are at work in his conception of presidential prerogatives. It harkens back to the small, entrepreneurial model of what it takes to be a president and what it takes to be a commander in chief of American society. In some measure, it is reflected in Carter's reduction in the scale of the presidency from imperial pretensions to domestic proportions. This is not a presidency that can respond, given the Vietnam antecedents, to large-scale international involvements. The discussion of the Carter presidency is, by fiat, a discussion of a United States much less willing to deal with these larger issues. Here again the vision of a southern fundamentalist, coupled as it is with an engineering entrepreneur, better fits a model of America as something small, as something within a society, rather than as a steward of the world. The decision with respect to limiting foreign policy initiatives is indicative of a decreasing sense of what America can do in the world, not in terms of a consciousness of geopolitical limits, but rather in terms of the limits of consciousness of this kind of traditional religious belief coupled with a small, entrepreneurial imagination.

LIPSET   Carter is a religious man and an engineer. I suggested earlier that engineers believe in solutions. I once mentioned this to an orthodox rabbi. He said "remember that religious people also believe in solutions. A religious engineer has a double proclivity toward finding solutions." For a religious engineer, a solution is moral. People who oppose the "solution" are opposing both expertise and morality because they are selfish. They reject the solution from the point of view of a special interest—of labor, of business, of Jews—and that is wrong.

Carter, like Lindsay, came into office believing that if a special interest tried to block him, he could always appeal over their heads to the people. The author of an article in the *New York Times Magazine* about Tip O'Neill, the speaker of the house and leader of the congressional Democrats, noted in February 1977, a month after Carter took office, that the president reacted to O'Neill's advice about the need to compromise with various groups in Congress with the comment: "Oh, don't worry about that. I had the same problems with the legislature in Georgia and got around them by appealing to the people over their heads." Tip O'Neill commented to the writer: "Carter is the only president we've got—and I've got to help him." Other congressmen are not as generous.

Back in February, also, one of the most distinguished Washington correspondents agonized over Carter's lack of understanding of the way Congress operated as a place in which policy was made through compromise, trade-offs, and by building coalitions. He noted that Carter had already antagonized some of the most powerful people in Congress. He commented privately that he wished he had the nerve to print a prediction, with which he agreed: that Carter had the potential to be one of the least effective presidents in recent American history. The journalist thought Carter came into office uninformed about how the federal government worked. He said that he would not print his opinion because Carter just might be lucky, so things might still work out. As he mentioned, crises must occur to produce significant trouble for a president; any given president could have the luck of Calvin Coolidge. Carter also could learn quickly.

To give credit where credit is due, there have been important moralistic elements in the Carter administration that are to be welcomed. He feels deeply about the race issue in South Africa. His famous *Playboy* interview, given months before the election, contained an unnoticed section in which the interviewer asked Carter about his record on civil rights. Carter said that he had to admit that his record in the past had not been good, that he was ashamed of it, and that he felt guilty he had not been involved in the struggles of the civil rights movement. He said that sometimes he thought that because of this he really should not run for president, but rather should spend the rest of his life trying to do something about South Africa. He brought this up before Andrew Young was in the picture as U.N. Ambassador. Carter, speaking spontaneously in this interview for *Playboy,* indicated that he had thought of becoming a missionary for civil rights in South Africa, that doing so would be the only way he could make up for not having taken the right positions in Georgia in the 1950s and 1960s. Carter probably never really seriously considered this, but the fact that he thinks or thought in these terms suggests that Andrew Young really speaks for him. The secret of why Andrew Young is not disciplined is that he is a spokesman for Carter's "Walter Mitty." When Young goes around denouncing whites, he is doing what one part of Jimmy Carter would like to do.

The human rights issue is another moralistic one in which Carter is on the side of the angels. Its history is interesting. There is some evidence that suggests that human rights emerged as a fortuitous campaign issue taken over from Jackson. Carter made some vague statements about defending human rights abroad without thinking through their full implications as part of a foreign policy. Immediately after he took office, an underling in the State Department issued a statement criticizing the Soviet Union on human rights. Carter's preelection statements were his authorization. There was some protest about this, and the State Department initially tried to downplay the position. They soon discovered that backtracking would be even worse, that human rights is a popular issue. The human rights issue developed a momentum of its own. The idea is too good and has had too much impact to be put back into the box, even though a lot of State Department personnel feel that it ought to be. If Carter is to be given any criticism for his position on human rights, it is for a selective application, for correctly criticizing the unsavory record of whites in Rhodesia and South Africa yet ignoring the situation in many other African states in which minority black tribes severely oppress majorities belonging to other tribes.

By raising the human rights issue, Carter has been able to do something I would not have anticipated. He has returned to the United States moral leadership on the international scene that it had lost as a result of Vietnam. One would have thought it would take a long time after Vietnam before the United States could speak out in moralistic terms to other countries, before it could again become the leader of a struggle for democracy, decency, and the like. Yet Carter has accomplished this. The Soviet Union has been forced on the defensive by the human rights issue. It has had an equally dramatic impact elsewhere. I was told by a former high official in the Indian government that the reason Indira Gandhi went to an election was the human rights issue. She was placed on the defensive by Desai, the then leader of the opposition, who made much of Carter's position on human rights. Regimes in a number of countries have modified their repressive policies. The statements that people have basic rights contained in the charter of the United Nations and the Helsinki Declaration sound like campaign rhetoric. Yet peoples, societies, and nations have to legitimate themselves. The Soviets and other dictatorships signed papers that they assumed were empty words. But suddenly, the

United States and other western nations began to stress the need to live up to these agreements. People have a right to emigrate, to a public trial, to speak freely. One of the most significant things to happen in recent years is the way that this emphasis on abstract ideals has actually led some of the most authoritarian governments to modify their policies. I am sure Jimmy Carter did not anticipate these consequences when he first raised the human rights issue during the campaign, but he certainly deserves credit for what followed.

Carter's moralism resembles that of Woodrow Wilson's, a comparison that may not seem encouraging to those who know American history. Moralists can be easily riled. Moralists, convinced they are right, that they stand for virtue, become righteously angry at the selfish people who oppose them. Congressmen report occasions in which Carter has become visibly angry at some of those who said they were not going along with something he proposed. I suspect that behind the smile that is so easily put on and off and clearly has no relation to his actual feeling is a man who is dangerous to counter. He may not have a written "enemies list," but he is the kind of person who, one suspects, remembers his "enemies."

HOROWITZ   When you speak of the human rights issue it reminds me of Hegel's remarks about Rousseau and the problem of general rights. One of the characteristics of the bourgeois consciousness is its ability to see human rights in an abstract, legalistic framework. Voting rights and migration rights fit in well with this concept of human rights. That is why the United States can develop a clear policy toward South Africa, Chile and Soviet minorities. Human rights translates into a democracy of numbers. But when economic considerations become primary, the name of the game changes. What is Carter going to do or say when 3½ million whites are compelled to yield their domination to 9 million blacks in South Africa? As George W. Ball recently asked: Will he send the whites darkly into the night, or will he support minority rule in the name of controlling communism? Human rights can mystify decision making if they are not viewed in concrete terms.

In point of fact, the human rights issue cuts two ways. Indeed, it has thrown the Soviet Union into a political lather. Simultaneously, it has also softened the American approach to Western Europe. It has conceded a kind of limited legitimacy to Eurocommunism because it now holds open the possibility of human rights. The human rights issue then has the same problem within it as does any other general moral position. We may argue for human rights while at the same time relinquishing concrete structural advantages to "our side" that stem from the present balance of power. Is Eurocommunism, for example, acceptable because it offers the possibility of maintaining human rights? Or is it unacceptable because it is, after all, still based on authoritarian political premises and economic premises? This is why people like Henry Kissinger have urged a careful reconsideration of the human rights strategy. It is not so much that he applauds détente as that he fears a tactic that spills over into a general principle—one with dire consequences for the United States and not just the Soviet Union.

When you translate this concept of human rights into an economic equation, what is left? One of the problems with all general moral categories, not to mention moral-centered politics generally, is that the equation, the balance, becomes more important than the absolute empirical analysis. We can hardly effect outcomes in the Soviet Union. But we can effect outcomes in Western Europe. At this level, are we to say that a rise of communist leadership in Spain, France, or Italy is permissible as long as basic political rights are observed? The human rights policy becomes problematic and tenuous because the United States, as a nation, represents a central economic system. Can it sit idly by and watch presumably human rights oriented communist regimes come to power and liquidate the basis of Western economic might?

The issue of human rights does not so much rebound to the credit of the president as raise serious problems concerning the possibility of the continuation of a presidential ideology based upon neoisolationism. I frankly do not believe that American society, given its present stratification system, would countenance a position based on the dissolution of American might and a dissolution of the Western comity on the basis of the human rights orientation of this or that communist regime. Whatever one makes of the human rights issue, it is far simpler to talk of it in terms of South African racial strife than European policies. The European aspect is the Achilles' heel of the West just as Third World aspirations are the Achille's heel of the Soviets. That is the rub in this grandiose moral scheme to engineer the world into a state of normative equilibrium.

LIPSET   I agree that Western Europe and the political future of Eurocommunism is going to have an enormous impact on the Carter presidency. But I do not know if American policy toward Europe and communism—the growth of Italian communism to be specific—will be determined so much by concern for human rights as by the realistic options available. For example, will the participation of communist parties in Western governments result in communist predominance in Europe as a whole? Some of the optimists, and there have always been optimists with respect to what the communists would do once they got into office, predict (hope?) that communist electoral victories will not lead to authoritarian regimes. Few believe that a predominantly socialist left government in France backed by the communists will be absorbed by the communists. Many socialists clearly understand the threat of communism. They would like to form a social-democratic government to make major reforms, but not to fundamentally change the basis of the system. The breakdown in the electoral alliance of the French left parties attests, in part, to the greater sophistication and strength of the French socialists. They, rather than the communists, benefited from the alliance while it lasted. The Italian situation is more difficult to predict because of the greater strength of the communists there, although capitalist enterprise might well survive for a long period under a communist-dominated government. But assuming that the Italian communists will destroy democracy or capitalism, what can the United States do to stop them?

It is hard to see what the president can do. For one thing, the power of the United States to use covert methods has been severely restricted. The exposés of the CIA have forced the agency to avoid such actions. This development, of course, has had some positive political effects in addition to eliminating some instances of outrageous behavior. With a weakened American resistance others have been forced to take responsibility for resisting communism. The Portuguese case is a good example. The Portuguese communists were close to coming to power, in spite of little popular support, because of backing by important elements in the military. Who helped prevent this occurrence by giving the principal opponents of the Portuguese communists money, people, and other aid? It was the social-democratic governments of Europe. The Portuguese socialists were the strongest opponents of a communist seizure of power. They received considerable support from their Swedish and German comrades.

With America out of the picture, other groups who do not want a communist takeover are forced to take action. This is good and necessary since the U.S. does not have the resources necessary to resist the communists all over the world. We do not have the means to stop events that we do not want to occur in Italy. We will not send in troops; the Sixth Fleet is not going to prevent a communist takeover. Covert or overt American participation in the domestic affairs of other nations can have only a boomerang effect, particularly in Europe. Ironically, the same inhibiting factors do not apply to the communists.

The inability of the U.S. to act effectively against the communists in Europe does not stem from Carter's commitment to human rights; it is an outgrowth of Vietnam, Watergate, and the CIA revelations.

There is another more serious source of American political weakness: the extent to which major segments of the intellectual and bureaucratic elites have lost faith in the moral superiority of Western democracy generally and of the United States in particular in the contest with the communist world. Vietnam was a turning point in the thinking of many antiwar Americans, who wound up favoring the victory of a communist state, North Vietnam, over the United States. A number of people who took this view and became active in the New Politics wing of the Democratic party hold high posts in the Carter administration, particularly in the foreign policy area. While none of them are communists, many prefer some form of social democratic or democratic socialist regime. The Vietnam experience convinced them that the United States should not support reactionary regimes in a contest with communists. Their conception of reactionary or repressive regimes includes many of America's traditional allies. This view leads them to favor a neutralist or isolationist posture for the United States, to look favorably on arguments justifying America's staying out of or withdrawing from conflicts between communist and noncommunist forces. Isolationism is obviously not the overall policy of the Carter administration, but isolationist sentiments are probably stronger within it than in any other administration since World War II. Ironically, many of our allies in Europe and Japan who publicly criticized the United States for fighting in Vietnam are now seriously concerned that the United States can no longer be relied on to defend their part of the world against communist takeovers. The American mood may change again, but, at the moment, Carter, as a post-Vietnam president, is not seen as a reliable ally in the fight. They are particularly worried about the influence on policy of the many McGovern New Politics Democrats within the government. Brezezinski, however, appears to be resisting them, and as a result of communist intransigence in Africa and in the SALT negotiations we have witnessed what appears to be the beginning the president's support of a tougher foreign policy in the second Carter year.

HOROWITZ   Quite apart from his enigmatic psychological characteristics, what we have in Carter is the first post-industrial president. This is the first twentieth-century presidency that does not appear to be directly tied to

American business interests. Hence, the human rights issue is both his strong and weak points by virtue of that fact. It is a marvelous issue for those who believe in the supremacy of politics over economics; or in the eighteenth-century political will over and against nineteenth-century propertied interests. We are in an odd moment where even capitalists whisper the word "capitalism." On the other hand, is the United States a capitalist civilization or is it not? Is this society to be known in terms of the politics of human rights or the economics of free enterprise? Or what shall be the mix the society will settle for? It might be that such polarized expressions are no longer necessary or even viable. Yet we should not become disingenuous on this point. Are we, for example, to renegotiate the nature of NATO or the Western Alliance as a whole? Just what has to be renegotiated in a human rights world? Perhaps if we renegotiate political power, the nature of the economic system will fall into place. Yet there is scant indication that the best and the brightest are addressing the issue of the nature of the American economic system.

In the light of such concerns as the human rights issue, our African policy, and our Middle East policy, at some point are we salvaging or condemning American labor and business interests? Is American foreign policy Machiavellian, a simple rubric and device to maintain traditional American aims, to save the world from bolshevism, despotism, or anything else we choose to dislike? Or is this human rights issue a ploy to announce in the most subtle manner the collapse of American business civilization? Whatever else the bourgeoisie or the bolsheviks are renowned for, it is not human rights. The issue admittedly has enormous magnitude that cannot be reduced to matters of strategy and tactics. In this country it may or may not wait the four-year period of time it takes to nominate or elect another president. At that level, I do not see much evidence that Carter or his administration have come to terms with the nature of the American economy and how it is affected by large-scale political issues, much less small-scale economic issues like tariff policies.

What I do see is an economic system without much regard for the political apparatus in Washington, and I see labor mechanisms, likewise, without much regard for the political system as it manifests itself in Washington. The economy continues to regard the polity as an impediment—except when the economy fails to sustain its profit-making goals. On the other hand, a Washington-oriented policy that has enormous consequences for the character and future of American civilization. Never mind the American *century*, which ended with its announcement in 1950. Does American *civilization* end in 1984? What you have emphasized in your remarks is the politics of continuity. Is there any element in this administration that somehow raises the spectre of the politics of discontinuity, or the politics of crisis?

One gets the impression that for Carter, like Robespierre, everything began anew (or was born again) when his administration took office in January 1977. There appears to be no sense of history, of continuity with the past, no harking back even to past Democratic presidencies such as was the case with Roosevelt, Johnson, and Kennedy. Even the human rights issue is raised as if there were no thirty-year United Nations agenda for the concrete expression of such rights in a series of quantitative indicators concerning everything from work to welfare. And the spectre of being doomed to repeat the mistakes of the past by virtue of Carter's colossal historical ignorance cannot be overlooked. That is why the potential for crisis is grave. We have crisis managers rather than social historians at the helm, or at least politicians lacking a historical vision; or for that matter, even a clear political party commitment.

LIPSET   These are interesting questions. To what extent does a democratic system think ahead? Clearly, the CIA had and still has the task of evaluating threats to American security around the world. If it is abolished, this function will have to be taken over by some other agency; some arm of government must assume these kinds of concerns. Outside government, there are few people other than a handful of social scientists paying much attention to the future prospects of the nation as a whole. Business concerns are like individuals: they prefer to believe the best is going to happen to them. They prefer optimistic scenarios and try to ignore negative symptoms.

The same generalization applies to countries. They also have a tendency to take a positive view. Those responsible prefer to think that the communists may not come to power, but that if they do, they will be "good" communists, nationalists, people with whom we can do business. Possibilities that may not happen are not on the front burner. In any case politicians prefer policies that will not be costly domestically. Currently, cost may be defined financially and electorally. Jimmy Carter made explicit campaign promises to have a balanced budget and to cut taxes by the end of his first term in office. It has always been obvious that he could not deliver on the first. But he has had to try to cut costs as much as possible. This has meant that when faced with a choice he generally opts for the least costly one, e.g., the cruise missile rather than the B-1 bomber; the withdrawal of troops from Korea; interpretations of Soviet and western communist intentions that downplay expansionist ambitions on their part. One reason that Carter appointed so many McGovernites in the foreign policy and defense areas, while totally ignoring the Jackson-Meany wing of the Democratic party, may be that the policies favored by the first group cost less than those advocated by the latter.

Business leaders, when they focus on profits, are even more likely than politicians to welcome foreign policy scenarios that imply greater opportunities for trade. They too would like to believe that cooperation with communist states will not harm American interests. In situations of crisis business firms optimize their investments, which may mean capital flight, getting out what they have, making preparations for withdrawal. They engage in optimistic discussions about negative outcomes, such as, if Italy does go communist, so what? The rest of Europe is stable, and Italy is an unstable society anyway. Andrew Young's blasé comments suggesting the United States should be unconcerned whether communist groups take over various African countries have met with little public criticism from the business community. There is a constant effort to see the positive aspects of a situation. One can do business with the communists. Gulf Oil is still operating in Angola. There will not be any concentrated resistance to communist takeovers from American business. The American labor movement is a much more active political foe of communism than business. Labor is much more ideological than business, more sophisticated in its awareness of the communist threat, still ready to help anticommunist labor groups abroad.

The shortsightedness of business, its readiness to sell the rope that will hang it for a profitable price (an aphorism attributed to Lenin), represents the ultimate failure of capitalism. If capitalism no longer can defend itself, if its leaders no longer can think of how to defend it, then it is indefensible—it has lost the battle. If the United States is the leading capitalist country in the world and no longer is willing or able to continue the role of leader of the free world, then, in a way, it has capitulated. I have been told by students of Japanese politics that Carter's announced policy of withdrawing troops from Korea has been interpreted by the conservative leaders of Japan as evidence that America can no longer be relied on as an ally, that they must begin to find ways of relating to China and/or the Soviet Union. But if the Western alliance is in trouble and vulnerable to internal crises, the Soviet Union and China face even greater difficulties. There is one big difference, however: communist systems, because of their authoritarian nature, have so far not been overthrown, no matter how bad conditions within them.

The fact that noncommunist authoritarianism is less stable than communism has almost been overlooked by liberal critics of repressive systems. In recent years Spain, Portugal, Greece, and India have become democratic societies; their dictatorial regimes proved unstable. Noncommunist dictatorships may last a long time, as did Franco's and Salazar's, but ultimately they collapse, since they are governments of aging cliques or juntas, not of charismatic parties. Communist regimes, with all their inner tensions, are able to maintain their authoritarian character, though at a high price to their subjects. The Soviet Union is an enormously inefficient, highly stratified, bureaucratic society whose ability to provide its people with a decent standard of living or to produce and operate efficient modern military equipment—planes, tanks, rockets, missiles—is far inferior to ours. But these facts do not affect the political situation in most of the noncommunist world, All nations harbor major social evils—racism, poverty, restrictions on freedom of advocacy, and so forth. Reforms do not result in political stability, for improvements in real conditions generally lag behind "the revolution of rising expectations." And this lag serves today to undermine the commitment to defend the western status quo against those who promise to bring about a more humane and egalitarian nation, no matter how often such efforts elsewhere have resulted in oppressive reactionary regimes.

HOROWITZ   We have now gone far beyond what an American president can actually accomplish. The fact that you allude to the weaknesses of the Soviet Union and socialist regimes is a kind of clutching at straws. They are indeed having their problems and we are having our problems. We may be presiding over the end of the Western world, or a dominant Western society; or we may be heralding a new century of human rights. Even when you speak of right-wing regimes being unstable in Portugal, Greece, and Spain, you are talking of European civilization. However, this does not have much influence upon the Third World, where tendencies toward militarization continue to overwhelm trends toward democratization. To be sure, a Third World that includes Amin's Uganda and Desai's India is not susceptible of easy definition, much less quick solutions. Yet the potency of military regimes to prevail in places where human rights—economic or political— are minimal is troublesome.

To return to our subject, the American presidency, if in fact Carter has the mind of a moralist and the soul of an engineer, both elements of which are goal-oriented and solution-prone, we have a petit bourgeois presiding in the

White House over the dissolution of the bourgeoisie. Nothing in what Carter says or does will forestall that eventuality from taking place. Whatever is wrong or not wrong with the Soviet Union and socialism, the United States is at a peculiar moment in time. It will be interesting to watch how interests, classes, sectors, labor, and management react to real-life events, such as the actual transfer of power in the Panama Canal Zone, a possible resumption of military hostilities in the Middle East, all-out racial struggles in South Africa, a decisive electoral victory for the communist parties of Italy or France. What would happen to our foreign policy in a world that would convert the rhetoric of human rights into the reality of a basic shift in world forces? Power is concrete. Rights are ultimately a translation of absolute power into shared power and, finally, powerlessness. Ultimately, if every person is to count as one—no more and no less—we are speaking of a negation of presidential power as well. But this might be more of a long-run discussion than either of us are equipped to foresee.

LIPSET   While all these are important questions in the long run, a long run that is not so long, I am not sure that these are questions that will come up in Carter's first term, which may very well be his only term. Events in Panama will, of course, affect the situation, but authority over the canal will not shift for some time. The white regime in South Africa is likely to last a bit longer than the Carter presidency. About Italy I will make no predictions, but it is not inconceivable that the confused status quo there will continue, that the Christian Democrats will stay in office supported by the communists for some years to come. Carter and his human rights rhetoric may continue to serve as a substitute for specific policies in many parts of the world.

HOROWITZ   So rhetoric preserves us from reality at least for the next two years.

LIPSET   This may be all that is left.

IV. DEVELOPMENT

LIPSET Some of you may know that we want to shift the topics a bit, but we will be continuing with some of the same emphases, while treating problems of developing societies and following up our earlier discussion on the problems of equality and inequality in the international world, particularly America's relationship to the Third World.

We have to admit that the topic of development and America's concern with it involves an inconsistent picture. In the decade immediately after World War II there was enormous optimism and a sense of promise with respect to the less-developed or underdeveloped world. The great colonial empires of Britain, France, Belgium, the Netherlands, and the United States had all come to an end. Most of the new states created democratic systems modeled on that of their former metropolitan country. When the United Nations was founded in San Francisco in 1945 it had 50 member nations, all the independent states of the time. It now has something on the order of 150 members. The extra 100 countries were almost all colonies or dependencies in 1945, so that real progress has been attained as suddenly all these countries arrived at independence, at self-government, at control of their own destinies.

But almost all these countries were poor, and in order for them to take off, to begin to develop economically, it was necessary for us to recognize that they would have to be assisted. Many people in this country, in the universities and government, became development experts (or tried to become experts). Political scientists dealt with political development, economists with economic development, to some extent, sociologists with problems of social change and social structure. There were a myriad of books written by people in different fields analyzing Third World problems and projecting how development would take place. Today, three decades later, the picture is a much less happy one. For one thing, though the countries that became independent are still, for the most part, independent, the hopes many people had that these countries would form democratic polities simply were frustrated.

In Africa almost all the countries have authoritarian regimes. Only about two or three tiny African countries still have competitive elections, a free press, and free discussion. The Latin American nations, which have been independent since the nineteenth century, also are almost all dictatorships. Those nations, like Chile and Uruguay, which had enduring electoral democracies for many generations, are no longer free. And for the moment there are only two major political democracies in South America: Colombia and Venezuela. The Arab world is characterized by dictatorial regimes in its twenty countries. The one Arab country that was relatively free, Lebanon, is a catastrophe. Asia, though predominantly authoritarian, presents a less gloomy picture, as India has returned to competitive politics and Pakistan is struggling to achieve them.

If one looks at problems of economic change and growth, the picture is about as bad. There are some countries that have done relatively well, such as South Korea, Taiwan, and the Ivory Coast. A few Latin American countries, like Brazil and Venezuela, have done better than others. Some countries are fortunate in having oil or other resources, which have given them greater capacity for growth. The phenomenon that I already touched on briefly, the neo-Malthusian problem of population growth outstripping resources, has become a major problem for some, although not all these countries. As we start thinking about problems of development today, we must begin by lowering our expectations from those we established in the decade after World War II. It is necessary to rethink our whole conception as to what is possible, what the relationships of the less-developed countries are and should be to the Western world, to the communist world, and to each other. Some now talk of a Third World and a Fourth World, differentiating according to available resources and wealth levels.

The first problem to deal with here is why the optimistic expectations went wrong. The answer is easier on the political side than on the economic one because the answer in part for the political failure is the economic one. Namely, these countries are poor, the overall majority of the population in each is poverty-stricken, only a tiny minority are wealthy, and only a small group are middle class. Attempts at democracy have been frustrated by the fact that the resources available to the governing elites and to the dominant parties are too few to effectively meet the demands of the electorate. Hence, in those countries opposition groups are viewed by incumbents as irresponsible, as promising things that cannot be delivered considering the available resources of the country. The governing elites simply cannot produce the kinds of payoffs that are anticipated or expected by people aware of the existence of an affluent modern world where things are different.

Contemporary underdeveloped countries face greater difficulties than less developed nations did two centuries ago, when the United States became independent of Britain, because there is now one world in terms of communication. This was not true, of course, even one century ago. Today, peasants in Thailand, Bangladesh, or Peru have transistors. Even if they are illiterate, as most of them are, they have some exposure to the fact that abysmal poverty and short life spans are not the state of most people everywhere in the world. They are aware that revolutions have taken place elsewhere. They often obtain exaggerated accounts of the improvements that have occurred elsewhere. The transistor, in effect, gives them access to blandishments about opportunity. The revolution of rising expectations reaches all, so poor people no longer accept the proposition that they have to remain poor. They do not want their children to be illiterate. The governments of most of these nations, however, have not been able to do much to improve the lot of most people quickly. Hence, the regimes are vulnerable to opposition attack, and the collapse of democratic regimes follows. This is not to say that most of the governments that turned dictatorial or were succeeded by authoritarian regimes had good intentions, or that they would have done well had they been allowed a sufficient period of time to develop long-range programs without being subjected to competitive pressures.

If we consider the factors conducive to economic growth and the reasons that steady growth has not taken place, we enter a more controversial area. On one hand, many people, particularly in various less-developed countries, would put the primary responsibility for the lack of economic development on the dependent relationship between these countries and the wealthier, more-developed countries. They would argue or contend that the LDCs are exploited economically, that the developed, wealthy industrial countries use them to get raw materials and labor cheaply, while insisting on high rates of profit on finished products. It is argued also that exploitative relationships with the more well-to-do nations have hampered development or even have created negative growth rates in some countries.

Others contend that this thesis is false. They point to the fact that some countries that have had dependent relationships in trade and investment with developed countries have prospered. Joseph Schumpeter pointed out years ago that the United States was in a typically dependent relationship with Great Britain and Europe for a long period in its early history, one comparable to that of contemporary LDCs; yet it developed. It is noteworthy that Canada, Australia, and New Zealand had comparable relationships to Britain before 1930, similar to those that Argentina, Uruguay, and Chile had at the same time. All six were affluent agrarian societies, exporting grain, beef, and, to some extent, dairy products to Britain. Canada, Australia, and New Zealand continued to grow and became wealthy industrialized countries with high standards of living, while the South American nations have moved backward, relatively.

The story of Japan may also be included in the argument. It is the only country outside the cultural and economic sphere of the Western world that has been successful economically. It now has a per capita income higher than that of a number of European nations and Britain. Yet Japan for a long time experienced a typical dependent relationship with more-developed nations, a status to which it was tied even more firmly following World War II. The fact that various dependent countries developed while others did not is presented as evidence for the argument that a dependency theory does not totally or even largely explain the economic failures of the LDCs, that part of the answer lies in their domestic or internal relationships, institutions, and values.

To now turn to the Second World, the communist world, it is important to recognize that most communist countries (there are about fifteen or sixteen) still fit into the category of less-developed countries. One of the ironies of communist experience is the fact that communism has not taken power on its own in any industrial society, though some of the countries conquered by the Red Army after World War II are industrial. The communists have attempted to industrialize the nations they have taken over, beginning with the Soviet Union. The Soviet Union certainly has become much more industrialized in the sixty years the communists have ruled it, and some will argue that the only effective road to industrialization requires socialist authoritarianism and planning, particularly the willingness to exploit the present generation for the future of a country.

To develop, to grow, a country needs investment, and apart from foreign investments, the only alternative is to take a large surplus of the existing production and use it for investment purposes rather than for raising the standard of living of the present generation. This is what Stalin did. But such policies can be quite unpopular—they involve taking from and underpaying the peasantry. In the Soviet Union peasants were underpaid for their farm goods, an action that required the use of troops. There was considerable violence in the Soviet countryside. If a country wants rapid growth, then reliance on force seems the only way to break up recalcitrant social structures in order to secure economic progress in less-developed countries. But this thesis is countered by the argument that the communist societies, once established, have become intensely bureaucratic; that bureaucracy ultimately becomes a drag, is economically self-destructive. The rate of growth declines, as it has in the Soviet Union today. There is considerable evidence that the Soviets have a very inefficient economy, however well it may have done in the past. These are some of the major developments and issues.

HOROWITZ   I will start from the assumption that the problem of growth is one of history and structure, not of pessimism or optimism. The more I look at this problem of developing areas and development, the more I am impressed by the fact that there are now three stable forms of political life in the world.

The first basic form, of course, is the capitalist mode of production in which economic variables are in fact fundamental. These are not just matters of class, status, and power. To look at Western Europe is to look at a system based on economic power, on economic classes contending for power, and on state apparatuses that are relatively weak. Perhaps the entire capitalist ethos can be summed up in the proposition of Bentham, "That government governs best that governs least." The first basic form of political life, that "hands off" the economy attitude, permits a Smithian world to emerge in which the hidden hand of providence divinely orders the relationship between people so that a balance of supply and demand is struck.

Whether you look at capitalism from the point of view of the London School of Economics or that of the utilitarian school, you essentially have a world of economy directing the society. And it is perfectly natural and realistic to talk about capitalism and Western European growth in terms of economic models. That is the alpha and omega of what capitalism is all about. Opportunity, supply, demand, a marketplace that regulates, and the whole notion of self-government. That is the capitalist style of development, not just its substance. When you talk about socialist models of production—socialist styles or substances of development—a funny thing happens on the way to the forum. All of a sudden the state or the polity becomes very important. The problem of mobilizing large numbers of people in areas that have to play catch-up becomes significant.

Socialism is not the advance announcement on the part of a vanguard group that the future will have more equity, precisely because equity is not guaranteed by providence. That is to say, the contentions of Marxism, three volumes of *Capital* and a fourth on *Theories of Surplus Value* notwithstanding, are directed at capitalist arguments of the automaticity of growth: that growth is not automatic, and certainly equity and growth are not identical. So you need mechanisms of regulation. And you do not only need state tinkering, you need to capture state power. By 1859 Marx was clearly talking about the seizure of power, about the political dominance of the system as a precondition of economic growth. What you have, then, within the socialist model, is a careful rereading of economic history. There is a realization that revolutions are largely defined by political acts and not just economic facts.

The end of the medieval period in France is dated about 1715. The French Revolution was 1789. That revolution is dated by the political overthrow of the Bourbons, not with the end of feudalism. The end of serfdom in Russia took place by 1860 or 1865 (there is some debate on what year exactly) but no less than fifty to seventy years prior to the Bourgeois Revolution of 1905 and the April and October Revolutions of 1917. When we talk about the Bolshevik Revolution or the Russian Revolution, we are not talking about the economic end of serfdom. The Meiji restoration-ism in Asia ended a good deal before the Shogunate be-came militarized and seized power, so that there was a disjunction between economic interpretations that were re-markably capitalistic in character. Adam Smith was the real economic determinist, and the Marxian socialist vision was highly politically deterministic.

The history of socialism is the history of the organization of the overthrow of a regime by a party for the purpose of political hegemony, to guarantee a kind of equity that eco-nomic life by itself does not guarantee. That is the real basis of all socialism. If you do not talk in terms of seizures of power, party apparatuses, and the organization of the society for political and economic ends, then you are just talking about the continuation of the old system under another name. As we entered the Third World of the twen-tieth century after 1945, what happened? Everything and nothing. Nothing in the sense that if you look at the new nations, especially in Africa and Asia, and some of the older nations of Latin America, increasingly you do not have the adoption of a multi-party democratic system but, rather, an adoption of the Leninist formulation of state power based on the model of single parties and party discipline, where decision making is arrived at through inner-party contention.

The world did not wait for Lenin to come along with this formula of party centralization. The Mexican Revolution institutionalized it in the years 1910–1920; the Kemalist

Revolution in Turkey also institutionalized party central-
ism quite independent of the Bolshevik seizure of power.
But clearly, as you move on in the twentieth century, the
formula in Africa at the political level is single-party van-
guardism, socialism of the whole nation and the whole
people, and the organization of society politically along Leninist lines. But the economies of those new nations are not
socialist, as in Eastern Europe or the Soviet Union, but
highly capitalist and competitive in the neo-Keynesian
sense. The marketplace economy is retained in these nations. New class formations are maintained, even stimu-
lated. Even now this process continues. In the Middle East,
for example, the emergence of oil politics has not led to
socialist economies but to the creation of OPEC as a new
player within the capitalist world. The Third World demands economic redistribution within the terms of what
some call state capitalism. They are willing to play energy
politics, but they also want the kind of commodity arrangements and class differentiations that presumably
stimulate competition.

Thus, the Third World has a dominant economic component that must be characterized as capitalist and a political
component that is strongly socialist or Bolshevist; or, in
other words, what you have is a Mexican standoff. Both the
economic and the political components have certain weaknesses that limit their capability to dominate. The great
strength of the political sector is that revolutionaries have
made this socialist marriage with capitalism not only feasible but largely successful. Those in economic/bureaucratic
structures, the Keynesian wing we will call it, argue the case
for developmentalism. In part, because of their training
under the old colonialists, they know what they have to look
for; in part too they know that the revolution takes a day
and development a millennium. Their tantalizing strength

is that they know how to organize society for economic ends. They do have a weakness: they are the unique residual sector of the colonial inheritance.

Under such conflicting circumstances, an entirely new social system emerges: namely, the military state, not as a war-making machine but as that group that uniquely represents the nation as a whole in the process of development and political integration. Rather than something we ought to bemoan or be too concerned over, the military is, in fact, an organizing premise without which the Third World cannot work. What we have, therefore, is an entire paradigm characteristic of the Third World, but not characteristic of either European socialism or American capitalism. And that paradigm is the military-bureaucratic state functioning like a surrogate class to maintain levels of order, levels of autonomy, and levels of integration within the national system.

That mobilization of the population is the unique contribution of the military is shown by the fact that country after country has turned to the military. There are weaknesses within this military model. It is very costly, and it incorporates all sorts of tensions and pressures. But the pattern of development in the twentieth century represents an entirely new paradigm. It is the military—not entrepreneurship, not values, not the traditional conventional rhetoric inherited from North American economic scholarship— that functions as an independent variable. As such, it is entirely unique in terms of the social organization of the Third World societies. We must come to recognize that the Third World is not, as the socialists claim, a world transition to socialism, nor is it as the capitalists claim, a world that is evolving new forms of class formation and hence joining the rest of the entrepreneurial world, but that it is a system unto itself—an entity real and permanent in our world. When we appreciate the permanence of Third World innovations, we will have a much better idea of the political dynamics of the developmental process.

LIPSET   I agree with much of what you say about the military regimes and the role of the military. One problem in this discussion is that we are talking about the regimes in ninety to one hundred countries on four continents, and the reality—the variation among them—is more complex than can be suggested here. This is the case particularly with respect to the military. The pattern described by Professor Horowitz is true for many countries, but it is not valid for every one of them. The military in different countries often has quite different orientations. In Peru there is a military regime that is perceived as leftist, as indicated by the kind of economic system it appears to favor. In Chile, Brazil, and Argentina the military regimes are thought of as rightist, as reflected in their alliances with conservative civilian groups and their economic programs. In the Middle East the Kemalist regime in Turkey, and Nasser's in Egypt, had leftist ideologies and were also based on the military. The army of the most enduring rightist dictatorship of modern times, that of Portugal, ultimately turned leftist.

Marxist theory, which you mentioned, does not help much, because Marx assumed that socialist revolution and planning could only occur in highly industrialized countries. Today Marxism is the label attached to a set of political slogans in the Third World—that is, "Marx" as a name. "Marxism" as a term has become a banner or flag by which a party or regime proclaims its dedication to benefiting the people against the well-to-do, to creating a more egalitarian society, and to its hostility toward the part of the world defined as imperialist. The sociological and economic theories of Marxism are inapplicable to the Third World, for all schools of Marxism, following Marx himself, assumed prior to 1917 that socialism only had meaning in a postindustrial society. Socialism, it was contended, could only come about in an advanced industrial society on the verge of abundance and super affluence—where the workers are the majority of the population, so that when the socialists take power, they would represent a majority class.

It was completely unthinkable to Marx that socialism could exist in a preindustrial agrarian society. He denounced those who suggested such a course as utopians, but the reality has been that regimes that call themselves socialist or communist have come to power only in preindustrial societies. Marxism as a sociological theory—as a theory of development—has absolutely nothing to say about such a possibility, except to insist along with Rosa Luxemburg that it must be a sociological monstrosity. Socialism and Marxism have simply become the terms by which the rulers of these societies legitimate authoritarian, exploitative state rule, both in the communist nations and in those noncommunist Third World countries that call themselves socialist and Marxist.

One of the basic assumptions of Marxism with which other sociological theories agree is that the poorer a country—the greater the economic scarcity—the more unequal is its stratification system. Extreme inequality is a function of a low level of development. It is also inherent in any effort to develop rapidly by extracting surplus labor (capital) from the poor. Following this assumption, it follows that the commitment to rapid development in poor countries will produce and sustain a great deal of inequality. Inequality can take different forms. We think of inequality in Western society primarily in terms of inequality of wealth; but there is also inequality of power. Power is much less equally distributed in the less-developed countries today than in the more-developed ones.

In nations such as the Soviet Union, China, Uganda, or Brazil, there is a highly unequal distribution of power. Power is concentrated in the hands of a small power elite that controls all avenues to influence and distribution of resources. It also follows that over a period of time the dominant power groups will take onto themselves and their families various social and economic privileges, much as the ruling elite of the Soviet Union has done. In seeking to anticipate the future of these countries, it remains to be seen whether and how they can develop and become industrialized. The authoritarian political institutions, the bureaucratized economies, the traditional social institutions in noncommunist LDCs, and the efforts of the "new class" of the communist countries to institutionalize its position do not augur a happy outcome with respect to the possibilities for freedom, greater equality, or, we may even add, economic development.

Whether much, if anything, can be done by people in the West, in the United States or Europe, to improve the possibilities is hard to see. Given the tremendous disparity in wealth that now exists between the average income standards of Americans or Western Europeans and those of the people in less developed countries, the West is simply not in a position to either lecture or advise these countries, politically or otherwise. Their elites are exploiting the gap between our wealth and their poverty to justify authoritarianism. The income gap becomes the base for raising as moral questions considerations of what is an appropriate price for oil, as with the whole OPEC situation. The OPEC countries doubled the price of oil and we were outraged. In their own defense, they have argued that we were buying oil from them at much too low a price. Some believe that we are not paying enough to the underdeveloped countries today for other natural resources.

On what basis does one set a price for oil? If it is fixed in relation to demand in an open market by buyers and sellers who do not conspire, there will be one price. If one creates a cartel or international trust, which is what OPEC has done, and simply sets whatever price the market will bear, there will be a different price. If one uses a labor or actual cost theory of value, then clearly the price that OPEC gets is much more than it should be, for labor does not cost much in these oil-producing countries. The world price is much more than the amount of money being paid to all the workers, the people involved in extracting oil. There is an enormous profit being made by the elites of the OPEC nations. This was true even at the old prices. The issue is not that of a fair price or moral price. It is a political decision as to how much the developed countries should pay for raw materials. Presumably the U.S. can pay more than it has in the past.

The issues, of course, are not just economic. Western countries are concerned with the relationship of the LDCs to the international alliance systems. There are obvious efforts to effect outcomes: to direct and move a country in a specific direction in relation to international political alliances. But most Western leaders and scholars have lost faith in their ability to advise Third World countries on the matter of development. Milton Friedman and his students have been asked for advice by some LDCs, and they advise them to go the full free market route. The irony, however, is that the Friedman school is dealing largely with countries that are already statist politically, being military regimes. There is a kind of incongruity in the image of advocates of a liberal, open-ended economy trying to operate in such close-ended regimes. The picture, while bleak, is also varied. Some countries have done much better than others. It is necessary to try to specify the conditions associated with success.

HOROWITZ   About eight years ago I did a paper entitled "Modernization, Mobilization, and Militarization" in which I was forced to conclude that the essential function of militarization in the Third World is to stimulate economic growth while maintaining a neo-Leninist political system. I went over that paper recently because I was trying to decide what had happened in the last eight years to either revise downward or upward that kind of thinking. There has been a continuing pressure toward achieving economic growth through military means, the politicized use of the military. Brazil is certainly, as Professor Lipset has noted, a successful illustration of that. India has continued to develop its public sector military budget far beyond the dreams of Nehru, much less Mohandas K. Gandhi. But the constant thrust toward militarization does have as its touchstone economic growth, making those societies internally viable economically and externally viable politically. The remarkable thing about the military pivot throughout the Third World is its unique ability to prevent the undue penetration of nations by foreign sources or multinational firms.

We would do well to remember that we are dealing with societies where the middle sector, the entrepreneurial sector, is small. Where the entrepreneurial sector is relatively large, like in the southern tier of South America, it is corrupt. They do not pay taxes; they do not invest in domestic produce or enterprise; they trade in contraband goods. In other words, they are not the kinds of bourgeoisie that made the United States work. They are more like an aristocracy interested in the modernized results of industrial growth. That is why the Third World bourgeois pivot could not in itself create a base of take-off and growth; and that helps to explain the absence of a strong liberal ideology as well. Compare with that the absence of an infrastructure in which you have a well developed proletarian class and you can see the need for some kind of military pivot, the sort that prevails throughout the Third World.

Why was there no growth of a proletarian class? Why are the working classes of Latin America, Asia, and Africa relatively small? Aside from the traditional factors of agrarian constraints, the answer is the intensity of the capital-intensive nature of modern industrial plants. In order to produce one million tons of excellent rolling steel in Brazil in the Volta Redonda region (that is, in the central coastal tier of Brazil) you need about ten thousand laborers working one week. To produce iron ore in Pittsburgh in 1890, or in Birmingham, you needed a labor force twelve times that size. So in the Third World you cannot have, as you had in Western Europe or North America, an enormous factory proletariat becoming politically involved and mobilized. To talk about the aristocracy as even remotely having the capacity to rule a modern state is to do an injustice to history. For that reason all those national regimes of independence emerged. The aristocracy had no need for the hypothesis of national identity.

Clearly, the peasantry has little capacity to rule; it is a class that can hardly be mobilized. So the military thrust is a function of hard political and economic realities, and it is largely successful. It would be a mistake to deny or discount relative degrees of stability and economic growth achieved under this pattern of military tutelage. To be sure, there remains an enormous problem. Even if you can create authentic military-style revolutions, the authenticity of the revolution does not guarantee its autonomy. Often, military regimes are incapable of autonomy even when they are vigorous in its pursuit.

Take the case of Cuba and the USSR. The current total indebtedness is over $4 billion. That indebtedness is higher, even adjusting for inflation and using 1959 as baseline economic data, than any indebtedness Cuba incurred to the United States prior to the present regime. The agony and anguish of the Third World is no longer connected with the authenticity or the actuality of revolution, or even the solidity of any given revolution. It has to do with the continuing pressures based on the fact that most Third World nations continue to exist as debtor nations within the International monetary system. In their underdeveloped condition they are frankly dependent on the larger powers, East and West. The Chinese now refer to the Soviets simply as imperialists, as the main military threat; no longer even as "social" imperialists.

This is indicative of a problem of bigness or smallness, which the Third World uniquely has to cope with. For it must deal not only with the big powers on an international scale but also with the growing differences between the big powers of the Third World and the relatively powerless cluster within that Third World. My colleague alluded to the balkanization of the United Nations, which has moved from

50 to about 128 nations. Well, the balkanization process takes place at the expense of big power influence. Those countries that have managed to resist big power domination—India, Canada, Australia, Brazil, and South Africa—will probably join the other nations as the most powerful within the twenty-first century. Multinational linkages mediate nationalist ambitions. Still, the process of militarization within the Third World is the essence of its developmental pattern. It has not been entrepreneurial, and it has not been proletariat. The recognition of that fact almost has to be pounded home lest we get caught up in traditional rhetoric about what Marxism means or what Marxism does not mean, or whether socialism as Marx described it is possible or not possible in less-developed countries.

Whenever one talks about socialism or developmentalism in less-developed areas, Marx's notion of the old society having to exhaust its potential for development is trotted out as a dark foreboding. In point of fact, Leninism does represent a reversal of historical economism. It recognizes, in some part, that Marx's formula was based on economic factors and that there are political mechanisms of mobilizing societies at very high cost. Perhaps these costs are too high for underdeveloped societies. We are dealing with an anguish of bodies, an anguish of lives in Third World development. How many lives is one willing to give up for how much economic development? The tradeoff is sorrowful; but development has always had a high price. We have not recognized this fact partially because we do not easily accept the possibility that the class struggle itself was intensified in the Western world precisely as a consequence of realizing the aims of development. Costs and benefits are really the issue. The empirical content of developmentalism in the Third World is no longer built on problems of political systems as slogans but rather on how much people are willing to pay for what services and for what goals.

LIPSET   The problem here is deciding where to concentrate and which methods work best. Given the problem of the low ratio of production to population that exists in many underdeveloped countries, it is necessary to cut the birth rate sharply. Japan did it following World War II. China has been equally successful in the last five years. Madame Ghandi sought to reduce the Indian birth rate by methods that led to her electoral defeat. Mexico, other Latin American and Caribbean countries, Egypt, Bangladesh, and much of Africa retain extremely high birth rates and hence must run fast just to stay in place in terms of per capita income.

There is a quite different problem affecting development politics: concern with national pride and power. Communist and military leaders particularly appear to have such concerns. National power is seemingly enhanced by industrialization, by possession of a big steel plant, by the ability to manufacture tanks, by having an atomic bomb. But in fact, many of these countries would do more good for their people, in terms of finding the optimum balance between productivity and needs of the population, by increasing agricultural productivity—having a green revolution—than by devoting resources to industrial growth.

Cuban history provides an interesting example. When Castro came into power, one of his complaints was that Cuba was a monoculture—it produced sugar sold to the United States and other countries. Supposedly, concentration on this crop reflected Cuba's dependency and exploitation. Castro and his advisors said that Cuban agriculture should become diversified. That would then make it less vulnerable to fluctuations in the international price of sugar. One of the things Cuba tried to do after Castro took power was to diversify by introducing other crops. It turned out that the most efficient thing Cubans could do in the world division of labor was to produce sugar. By producing and selling sugar efficiently, they could buy manufactured goods. The best way to enhance their income and standard of living was to grow more sugar, not less. The same kind of reality has even existed for the United States and Canada. Populist and other agrarian radicals in the great plains of Kansas and North Dakota, Saskatchewan, and Alberta would argue that the reason their economies were limited to growing wheat was that Wall Street, or Bay Street, was constraining them—eastern banks or industrialists did not want factories out in Saskatchewan, or Kansas, or North Dakota. But the populist and socialist governments that took power in these areas discovered there were good economic reasons why wheat was grown.

Nonindustrial agrarian societies resist operating within an international division of labor. They press toward economic autarchy. The military, particularly, is disposed to favor industrialization, to seek to build up what seems to be the basis of military strength, national power, and national pride. Thus, each country tries to imitate what other countries are doing. Many of the leaders of these countries, however, may do more to raise the standard of living, the way of life for their population, by increasing food production than by seeking to replicate within their nations the various sources of industrial power. The population problem some countries face is, ironically, a consequence of the fact that the form of modern technology most easily and quickly exported has been health technology, e.g., modern sanitation devices and immunization. But diffusing health technology abroad has served to raise the population growth rates way beyond those of the Western countries when they were developing economically in the nineteenth century.

The solution also is a technological one: contraception devices. We know how to stop population growth, and the Western world as well as Japan, Korea, and China have done so. But in many societies efforts to foster contraception run up against cultural values, value-related forces. Societies are quick to accept ways of prolonging life; yet some resist methods of preventing new life from being born. The best argument for reducing population growth is the Japanese experience. The Japanese were very poor compared to the West after World War II. Japanese per capita income increased not only because of economic growth, but also because the birthrate declined enormously. The Japanese have practically had a zero-growth rate for some time now. All their economic gains can go to investment and increases in the real standard of living since they do not have the problem of running fast just to stay in place.

The rapid growth of the GNP in Taiwan and South Korea is also, in part, a function of a sharp decline in birth rates. To tackle population growth is both a more difficult and more mundane strategy than institutional reforms. But two changes—an increase in the food supply and the discovery of new energy deposits—will drastically improve the situation in countries like Mexico and Nigeria. These seem much less ambiguous goals than creation of a new "socialist" society, but they can result in practical achievements in the immediate future.

HOROWITZ For the most part, you have to divide the world microscopically, less into aggregate numbers. When the concept of a Western hemisphere is invoked, Canada no less than Latin America must be included. As an area, we are talking about underpopulated regions of the world. We are talking about the Canadian population, which is now over twenty million. Twenty years ago it was eleven or twelve million. A lot of immigration has taken place. Argentina is vastly underpopulated. When one wants to talk about the metaphysics of demography, one has to be serious about the underpopulation problem in Argentina, Canada, and many of the countries of Latin America. Brazil is only now beginning to boom in terms of population numbers, and that country, equal in land mass to the continental United States, still has less than one half the population of the United States—110 million.

There are disadvantages as well as advantages to coming last in the industrialization race. Brazil cannot easily penetrate older export markets, so it must create internal markets for goods and services in an import substitution economy. But more important than the simple recognition that not every country in the world has a population problem like India or China is recognition that the correlation between high industrialization and high population has been noticeable throughout European history. In England, where relatively good data is available from the eighteenth and nineteenth centuries, the correlations between population and industrial growth are remarkably similar. Quite a few British demographers have pointed out that the highest periods of industrialization correlate quite nicely with the highest periods of population growth.

I am not trying to deny that there is a problem of population in India, China, or in Asia generally, but it is not simply an aggregate problem that is universal to the Third World as a whole. Nor should we assume the metaphysics of too many ecosystems advocates like Paul Erlich that a slender increase in the population causes an automatic corresponding decrease in GNP. It simply is not the case. And it is dangerously mechanistic, because if many of these countries are to develop and take off, the human resource factor is exceptionally important, especially in a country like Brazil, which has maintained, with the exception of a brief interlude in 1974, a heated growth rate of between 9 and 12 percent, a rate far in excess of its population boom. Beyond that, as you know from your own research, as countries develop Western types of affluence, the tendency toward reduced family size becomes much more pronounced, especially the tendency to have small family or integral family units rather than extended family units.

Family size reduction is compounded with industrialization. One of the anomalies in the kind of presentation we are being offered now, the green revolution, is that it offers us a continuing high boom in population growth. We know from the history of Western society that if you are really interested in population control you must have a high level of technical development. So industrialization is, in fact, the necessary correlate of the outcome you seek; namely, a more stable, steady relationship between GNP and population growth.

To argue, as the Population Council and the Ford Foundation often have done, that one can accept backwardness based on traditional agrarianism in terms of an international division of labor and, at the same time, have a reduction in population size is a kind of conceit on the part of advanced countries that is manifestly and categorically rejected by developing societies. To simply talk in terms of international divisions of labor is to guarantee that we will be taken seriously only as ideologists of an international distribution of wealth, which on the face of it is not equitable. Again, this argument reintroduces the zero-growth or limited-growth model, which does not offer any corresponding prospect of genuine international equality based on resource redistribution.

LIPSET   Clearly, I would like to make a few brief points. It is clear that there is considerable variation among the so-called Third and Fourth World countries, and, as noted earlier, one problem in this discussion is that we are trying to force into one mold countries that are quite different in everything from birth rates to rates of development of industry. The population pressure problem is not a general one, but it does affect a number of Third World countries. While it is true, as you say, that birth rates decline with industrialization and modernization, this has always occurred in the past—such phenomena may take two generations. Meanwhile, a tremendous jump in the number of mouths to be fed occurs.

QUESTION   I would like to get your reaction to the situation in the Middle East. It has been written that there will be a little war in the Middle East, and it will be to our interest, and to the interest of Europe, Israel, the Arab nations, and everybody except Iran. I wonder if you would comment on this.

LIPSET   I have not heard much talk of another war between the Israelis and the Arabs as a positive prospect. All discussions of the possibility have assumed that it would be disastrous for all concerned, except possibly the Soviet Union. I do not see how a war, another war between Israel and the Arabs, will benefit anybody. What good would a war do? It certainly is not going to bring about a durable peace. If anything has been learned from the four or five wars between Israel and the Arabs it is that these wars end up inconclusively. But even if Israel is allowed to go on much further than it has in the previous wars, I doubt that this would result in real peace. Victory for the Arabs would require annihilation of the Israelis, and I do not think that the United States or Western Europe would permit that to happen.

QUESTION Dr. Horowitz comments that development has been identified with industrialization, but in the next one hundred years industrialization for less-developed countries will become more difficult than present advanced industrial countries underwent in their development. Is it necessary because of limited resources and special energy resources to identify development with industrialization, or could a kind of agrarian development take place? Does agrarian development have to mean agrarian backwardness in an age where communication does not make it necessary for people to be together to be in communication with the modern world? Can sophisticated scientific information now be developed in the area of the biological and ecological sciences?

HOROWITZ My own thinking on development emphasizes industrialization because I was counterproposing and juxtaposing my own position with that of a number of colleagues, or former colleagues. Among these are men like David Apter and Daniel Lerner, each of whom has identi-

fied the developmental process in relation to modernization or the impulse to consume. My work, *Three Worlds of
Development*, is premised on the fact that development is
not the same as modernization; indeed modernization may
generate new forms of backwardness. It may yield high
differentiations between the urban rich and the rural poor
that obviate the very nature of the developmental process
itself. And the impulse to consume is not necessarily benefi-
cial to the development process. On the other hand, I am
not by any means wedded to the idea that development
simply means industrialization. Unlike people such as Robert Heilbroner, I do not believe that you can simply talk
about the developmental process as though it were isomorphic with industrialism. I do "tilt" heavily in that direction. One has to pay heavy dues to have the kind of developmental realities that people in less-developed areas
want. Those who are closest to my views among economists are Albert O. Hirschman and Gunnar Myrdal. People
in the agrarian sectors of underdeveloped areas have a
great demand for products of the advanced industrial nations. They want automobiles, and they want them now.
That part of the Lerner/Schramm hypothesis is correct.
There is instant communication between center and pe-
riphery nations. However, this is as much the problem as a
solution. It raises wants and expectations with no corresponding ability of the economy to meet such expectations.

It is the task of the state to create mechanisms that permit the best form of development given the resources available. The real problem is the concept of nationhood itself.
As the price of industrialization becomes higher, the world
cannot afford to have an international division between
those nations that remain agrarian and those that go industrial. Certain areas can evolve economies of scale in terms

of agrarian products rather than industrial goods, and should be encouraged to do so. But within the present context of the nation-state, that kind of international division is not possible. It is preposterous to assume that nations are going to accept economic rationality if it means military or political impoverishment and dependency.

A high amount of human suffering often accompanies parallel forms of industrialization, even when those forms may be superfluous in strictly economic terms. It is futile to think only in terms of economic reality in a world that is determined to create national and military rationality. And it is ridiculous to say that a nation should, in policy terms, or would, in empirical terms, restrict the nature of its growth to those aspects that are solely economically reasonable. Equity and equity-producing systems do not simply result from economic rationality, or many countries would accept the condition of agrarianism. In Eastern Europe agrarianism is a consequence of a tutelary arrangement with the Soviet Union. To deny that kind of tutelary arrangement ultimately means to challenge that kind of agrarian solution. If one were to argue that the advanced industrial societies should move toward agrarian solutions and maximize environmental arrangements so that you would have a lessening of tensions by the movement of both advanced and less-developed nations toward a kind of agrarian rationality, then you might be saying something that could be looked into seriously.

QUESTION   A recent development is the internationalism of American business and the growth of multinational business. Do you see any consequences of this in American values?

LIPSET   The growth of multinational, or as some people prefer, transnational corporations is an important phenomenon in the international economic picture. These companies are not agents of nor are they operating in the interest of any one state. They deal with national states as private companies interested only in how to optimize their own profits. We saw the effects of this in the Yom Kippur War during the oil boycott when various oil companies were clearly not trying to maximize American national interests. But I do not know how they affect our sense of nationalism. Should we stop thinking of Ford or General Motors as American companies because they operate in other countries?

I should indicate that I think the power of the multinational companies vis-à-vis other countries—or at least the image of them as a new kind of international ogre—is considerably exaggerated. Raymond Vernon, who has studied the oil situation, concluded that one reason for the rise in the power of OPEC was the political weakness of the multinational oil companies. The Arab countries started out with the assumption that these companies had enormous power, but almost every time they applied a little pressure the companies bowed and quaked. It has been suggested by people who have studied the situation that the Arab countries escalated their demands because the multinational oil companies turned out to be so weak in dealing with them. Some argue that if these companies had exercised some of the power attributed to them by the Arabs, they would not have been nationalized. These companies assumed they could not stand up to independent, even though weak nations. The power of the nation-state, when it is acting as a state, is very great.

QUESTION   Are things improving? Do we know how to develop less-developed countries? Aren't you defending inequality
when you try to explain its rationale?

LIPSET   The international situation cannot justify optimism; the reverse, if anything, is true. The spread of
knowledge about atomic weapon production in a world
marked by an increase in international terrorism holds
forth the promise of large-scale disasters. How, then,
should poor countries be developed? As I see it, the most
rapid way to develop such countries, if by development
one means raising the per capita standard of living, is by
increasing agricultural efficiency and cutting down the
birth rate. The other approaches will only enlarge the gap
between the wealthy and the poor. If you increase the gap,
the prospects for international terrorism, revolution, conflict, and ultimately, unresolvable conflict will grow.

We in the West read about and judge as crazy behavior
that the Cambodians are cleaning people out of the cities.
The Vietnamese are beginning to reduce urban populations. The Chinese have done this. The Asian communist
regimes appear to be moving away from the emphasis on
industrial development. Yet the Soviet Union made a
commitment to industrialization from the start. In order to
industrialize rapidly, they had to do two things. One was
to exploit the peasants by engaging in the famous "scis-
sors": appropriate labor and resources from the peasants,
use them for capital, refuse to pay the peasants the worth
of their goods, take the surplus value from the peasantry.
The other decision the Soviets made was to build up certain parts of the country while allowing the rest of the

country to remain backward and primitive. Large parts of
the Soviet Union are still extremely underdeveloped and
poor today.

The Chinese apparently—and I say apparently because
little is known about what goes on there in spite of all the
visitors—are taking a different road. Unlike the Russians,
they have chosen to emphasize agrarian development first.
They are not exploiting the peasantry for the sake of industrialization; they are not trying to build up one part of
the country and ignore the other parts. The Russians argue
that these policies are wrong. The Cambodians are seemingly following the Chinese model. The Vietnamese in the
Russian camp are more mixed or possibly uncertain.

The communists recognize that stratification is inevitable in their world. When most of that world lives in
poverty, it is impossible to have equality. As Marx argued,
in a world marked by poverty great inequality is inevitable. The people who have power will use it to maintain
wealth and privilege for themselves. What can be done
about it? To recognize that inequality exists and why it
does is not to defend it; it does not mean that you accept it,
but rather that you recognize that there is no way to have
an egalitarian world when on a world-wide scale equal
distribution means equal poverty. The problem remains
how to develop the less-developed countries. Clearly we
have not been doing a good job except among the already
developed countries and a few others that have joined their
ranks by solving this problem. I have to agree with what
Professor Horowitz said: that nation-states, and particularly the military and political leaders of nation-states, are
in a certain sense international egotists. They want to be
important, to possess the symbols of status, which, to a
nation, means steel mills and atomic bombs.

India's efforts to secure nuclear energy and the bomb make no sense except as fulfilling symbolic power needs. And yet, the Indian government went that route with materials and supplies that the Canadians gave them. This is the real world. To analyze the real world is not to make judgments that some things are or are not preferable although one may certainly exercise that option philosophically. People come to the conclusion that certain outcomes are more probable than others, such as a nuclear disaster. You can say that by making such statements I am rationalizing the situation, that I am defending it, because if one says something is highly probable, this justifies it when it does occur and makes it more difficult to resist. But the question still remains, which outcome is most probable?

To elaborate on the relationship between analysis, prediction, and personal responsibility, I would like to discuss a manuscript I recently completed dealing with the weakness of radical parties in America. It was first presented at a conference at Columbia University. I was dissatisfied with my first draft, feeling that I had nothing new to say. The chairman of the conference, Zbigniew Brzezinski, who has since moved to larger tasks, kept badgering me to submit a revised copy for publication for a book he was editing. Since I did not feel my contributions to be original, I decided to see what others had written on the subject. I read everything I could find, from the many comments of Marx and Engels, down through Lenin, Gramsci, Thomas, Harrington, and various academic specialists. One of the conclusions that increasingly emerges from this literature is that the American political system, particularly the placing of executive authority in the hands of one office, the presidency, makes it almost literally impossible—not just improbable, not just unlikely, but impossible—to build an effective third party.

Voters are constrained to choose between the two leading nominees for the office; support for lesser candidates
invariably drops away. Consequently, we have developed
a system of two coalition parties, within which the diverse
interests and ideological tendencies compete and bargain
with each other. As I noted in our first dialogue, we have a
covert multiparty system with each of the major parties
including groups that would otherwise be separate parties
if the United States had a different constitutional and electoral system. American parties, therefore, must be viewed
as coalitions that are not the equivalents of parties elsewhere. American political parties are not parties in the
European sense. American radicals, by attempting to build
a European-type party, have undercut their potential influence in this country. But radicals who seek to build a new
party have repeatedly stated that people who claim it is
impossible to create a strong third party are thereby justifying the existing two-party system. Of course, it is true
that to say it is impossible to build a third party discour-
ages efforts to build one.

But does such a conclusion necessarily involve defending the status quo? If it is true that a third party is impossible, and that there are alternative, possibly more effective
strategies, then the people who insist that radicals work
outside the two-party system are the ones who have ne-
gated the potential for political radicalism in America. The
issue is not whether rationalization or ideology is involved
in a social science analysis. Of course they always are. No
social scientist is free of his values and preferences when he
defines his problem, selects his data, and forms conclusions. But to reach particular conclusions is not necessarily
to prefer them. The social scientist may find himself in the
position of the physician who discovers that a patient has a
fatal illness.

The greatest of modern sociologists, Max Weber, understood and addressed himself to this issue, although for reasons I cannot understand he has been attacked by leftists as an advocate of value-free social science. Max Weber explicitly stated that whenever anybody talks about ethically neutral science, suspect him, for there is no such thing. And he went on to say that scholars whose research findings seem to support their own theories or "party line" on a particular problem should distrust these findings and not publish them or teach them to their students until they and others have checked them over carefully. He argued that results that are the opposite of what scholars would like to find are more likely to be correct. A good scholar, in Weber's opinion, should be much more ready to accept research findings that contradict his value preferences than ones that are congruent with them since we all want to find what fits in.

I am curious about a remark made by Professor Wilk that we were pessimistic yesterday but optimistic today. I feel just the opposite. Maybe we did not say so explicitly, but, on the whole, I think domestic conditions within the United States have been improving. All the students of social mobility agree that the rates of upward mobility have been increasing, that the less privileged have a greater chance to move into more privileged positions, up to and including the business elite, than did their parents or earlier generations. Recent analysts of income distribution, like Simon Kuznets and Morton Paglin, find when they control for type of family unit and for age that there has been a steady decline in income inequality from the 1930s through the 1970s. If government transfer payments are included as income, as they should be, then the decline in inequality is even greater. Those who insist that the distribution of income is not declining have ignored transfer payments and have not controlled for the fact that income varies sharply with age: the young and old have much lower incomes than the middle-aged. The situation of "minorities"—blacks, Hispanics, women, and homosexuals—also have been improving, though it remains bad compared to that of straight white males. And, as I noted earlier, we have more political freedom in the United States than ever before, while the rights of the accused are also in better shape.

Internationally, however, the situation has been worsening. None of us has talked about the danger of atomic war. But it should be noted that the existence of the bomb has delayed or hopefully prevented a war between the major powers. Without the bomb, World War III, fought with conventional weaponry, would probably have occurred some time ago. The bomb, however, is a dangerous reed on which to lean. Even if the existence of a deterrent does forestall war, it cannot work forever. And as possession of the "secret" spreads to different countries, somebody is going to throw it. When the point is reached in the not too distant future when bands of terrorists can get their own bomb, the possibility of nuclear war becomes a probability.

HOROWITZ   I will make my final remarks brief, but hardly painless. The same colonial powers that ruled at the beginning of the twentieth century continue to be preeminent. The character of the social order and of social systems has changed somewhat, but only as a consequence of two world wars. George Lichtheim, in a moment of deep sadness prior to his demise, said that these changes have come about only through many, many wars. We seem to have come out of the tunnel at the same place we entered it, certainly in terms of the distribution of power. If that is not a sad commentary on the misery of the twentieth century, then I do not know what is. We are so caught up in the rhetoric of social change that we sometimes ignore the reality of political and economic continuities.

On the other hand, there are indeed new players; the world is different than it was one hundred years ago. Karl Marx never thought about Africa or Latin America. Hegel limited Africa in his philosophy of history to one paragraph. The nineteenth century knew little about the varieties of peoples existing outside European civilization. Comparative anthropology hardly existed. Surely that has changed. The players, while they still have their preeminence, have a preeminence rather like that of a mosquito flapping its wings before expiration. The world is conceptually, at least, more expansive; it is much more rich; its physical size and global shape are more isomorphic. For the first time, the Copernican Revolution has reached the social sciences, or the historical sciences. The present Western arrogance and conceit, the amazing narrowness of what we consider conventional wisdom or culture is either in the process of being shattered or has been shattered. The meeting of East and West has already taken place; now it is joined by the meeting of North and South.

Equity is on the international agenda. But the dimensions of the problems are much more soberly considered than in the past. The potential for some kind of world order and world civilization, although it remains utopian, is at least plausible. I would like to believe, with Immanuel Kant, that world order and world law are possible. But part of me sees only the rise of the nation-state in more powerful and more prophetic terms. And one lives with that contradiction, with the legacy of a world in which one would hope to have some international order, and with the realities, which are a good deal less ambitious and less feasible. But that has always been the way, and I do not see that there is any reason for despair. It is rather that we must adjust our sight to the fact that the global victories we anticipated are much more fragmented than was initially expected. But living in a dangerous, partial world is nothing to be despairing about. After all, world order has its own contradictions. At some ultimate level it succeeds by liquidating individual rights and private initiatives. There are no magic formulas; slogans to live by turn out to be easier to die with. It is better to live between the crevices, in the cracks of theory, than on the hot coals of ideology—even well-intentioned developmental ideologies.

SEYMOUR MARTIN LIPSET

Elites in Latin America. New York: Oxford University Press, 1967. (Edited with Aldo Solari)

Emerging Coalitions in American Politics. San Francisco: Institute for Contemporary Study, 1978. (as editor)

Failure of a Dream?: Essays in the History of American Socialism. Garden City: Doubleday-Anchor Books, 1974. Rev. ed. Berkeley: University of California Press, 1979. (as editor with J. H. M. Laslett)

Political Man: The Social Basis of Politics. Garden City: Doubleday-Anchor Books, 1963.

Rebellion in the University. Rev. ed. Chicago: University of Chicago Press / Phoenix Books, 1976.

Revolution and Counterrevolution. Garden City: Doubleday-Anchor Books, 1970.

The Divided Academy: Professors and Politics. New York: Norton Library, 1976. (with Everett Ladd)

The First New Nation: The United States in Historical and Comparative Perspective. New York: Basic Books, 1963. Rev. ed. New York: Norton Library, 1979.

The Politics of Unreason: Right-Wing Extremism in America, 1790–1977. Rev. ed. Chicago: University of Chicago Press / Phoenix Books, 1978. (with Earl Raab)

IRVING LOUIS HOROWITZ

Ideology and Utopia in the United States, 1956–1976. New York: Oxford University Press, 1976.

Masses in Latin America. New York: Oxford University Press, 1970. (as editor)

Social Science and Public Policy in the United States. New York: Praeger Publishers / Holt, Rinehart and Winston, 1975. (with James Everett Katz)

The Knowledge Factory: Student Power and Academic Politics in America. Chicago: Aldine-Atherton Publishers, 1970; and Carbondale: Southern Illinois University Press, 1972. (with William H. Friedland)

The Rise and Fall of Project Camelot: Studies in the Relationship Between Social Science and Practical Politics. Rev. ed. Cambridge, Mass: Massachusetts Institute of Technology Press, 1974.

The Struggle is the Message: The Organization and Ideology of the Anti-War Movement. Berkeley: The Glendessary Press / Boyd E. Fraser Publishers, 1971.

The War Game: Studies of the New Civilian Militarists. New York: Ballantine Books / Random House, 1963.

Three Worlds of Development: The Theory and Practice of International Stratification. Rev. ed. New York: Oxford University Press, 1972.

NAME INDEX

Amin, Idi, 153
Apter, David, 183
Arendt, Hannah, 27

Ball, George W., 143
Banfield, Edward, 115
Beard, Charles, 23
Bell, Daniel, 52, 82, 126
Bentham, Jeremy, 164
Blumenthal, Michael, 112, 129
Bonadede, Dom, 109
Boulding, Kenneth, 40
Boyer, Neal, 120
Brown, George E., 129
Brown, Jerry, 23–24, 50
Brzezinski, Zbigniew, 110, 118,
    120, 129–30, 133, 147, 189
Bureaucrat, The, 122
Burns, Arthur, 128
Butz, Dean, 128

Caddell, Pat, 132
Cameron, Juan, 127
Capital, 165
*Capitalism, Socialism, and Democ-
    racy,* 51
Carter, Jimmy, 5, 9, 16–17, 97, 105,
    107–9, 111–14, 118–44, 146–47,
    149–51, 152–54

Castro, Fidel, 177–78
Cheney, Richard, 118
Coolidge, Calvin, 139
Crozier, Michel, 28
*Cultural Contradictions of Capital-
    ism, The,* 52

*Democracy and the Organization of
    Political Parties,* 29
Desai, Morarji, 141, 153
Dukakis, Michael, 23
Duncan, Dudley, 62
Dunlop, John, 111–12, 128

Eccles, Marriner, 128
Economist, 130,134
Ehrlichman, John, 111
Eisenhower, Dwight D., 13, 21, 102,
    128
Eizenstat, Stuart, 110
Ellsberg, Daniel, 37
Engels, Friedrich, 189
Erlich, Paul, 181

Figaro, 120
Ford, Gerald, 13, 17–18, 21, 23,
    112, 118–19, 128–29
Forrester, Jay W., 57n

INDEX